TESTIMONIALS

"Are certain 'absolutes' really that important? Only if you want a hugely successful business based on integrity and trust. Whether you own and/or lead a small business, large conglomerate or anything in between, this terrific book will equip you with 20 core, non-negotiable principles that will help you build a committed, happy and empowered team of people. Your customers will love you, and a very consistently high bottom line will be the result. If I may suggest, buy a copy of this book for all the leaders and future leaders in your life."

—BOB BURG, coauthor of *The Go-Giver*

"Sam Silverstein has, once again, given us all a gift of his insight and wisdom wrapped in the reality of a true-life success story. *Non-Negotiable* will change your thoughts, ideas, and actions which will change your life."

—JIM STOVALL, best-selling author, *The Ultimate Gift*

"As someone who's written about successful companies—both large and small—I have learned one thing: The principles of success are simple, but the execution of those principles is hard. The primary job of leadership is to clearly present and continually reinforce what their company stands for. In this book, Sam Silverstein shows how J. Pat Hickman and the team at Happy State Bank have done just that. Their principles are non-negotiable, meaning that they are firm, fixed, unwavering. And that is how you create a me will endure."

—ROBERT SPECTOR, cofounder of l
and autl

"As a person who has built four multimillion dollar businesses from the ground up, I can tell you without any hesitation the understanding and application of the principles in *Non-Negotiable* is what it takes to be successful. In fact I can't imagine anyone or any organization being successful without them. What I love about the book is the writer, Sam Silverstein. Sam is not sharing theory; he is sharing his heart, his passion, and his knowledge of what works from good old-fashioned sweat equity. You will love this book!"

—PAUL MARTINELLI, president of the John Maxwell Team

"Nearly every Hall of Fame athlete, nearly every revered musician or artist, nearly every prolific writer, and nearly every prosperous banker (and you could keep naming professions) will state unequivocally that he or she learned great lessons from someone in the same career field, and that most of those lessons crossed over into many other areas of their lives. *Non-Negotiable* is the story of Pat Hickman. It's a book that tells the story of a unique and highly successful businessman, but provides life lessons for everyone. Author Sam Silverstein has fully captured the spirit of Pat Hickman, and almost every page of *Non-Negotiable* proves why he has been so successful. Chapter 20, in particular, is a superlative list of how to live a great life. This book is not just about Pat Hickman's success, but how you, too, can learn and do what generates a high level of success in your life.

I suggest that you make reading *Non-Negotiable* non-negotiable."

—MARY MORRISSEY,
author of *Building Your Field of Dreams*

"This powerful message about the direct linkage between values and success should be practiced in every business."

—BRIAN TRACY,
author of *The Power of Self-Confidence*

THE STORY OF
HAPPY STATE BANK
& THE POWER
OF ACCOUNTABILITY

SAM SILVERSTEIN

Sound Wisdom
P.O. Box 310
Shippensburg, PA 17257-0310

For more information on foreign distribution, call 717-530-2122.

Reach us on the Internet: www.soundwisdom.com.

ISBN 13 HC: 978-0-7684-0724-2
ISBN 13 Ebook: 978-0-7684-0725-9

For Worldwide Distribution, Printed in the U.S.A.
 2 3 4 5 6 7 8 / 19 18 17 16 15

DEDICATION

To Sharon Miner

Everything changed when you called. Thank you for your faith
and guidance in making this project the very best it could be.
You are right, it really does matter what you believe.

ACKNOWLEDGMENTS

Thank you to everyone associated with Happy State Bank who took the time to be interviewed. To the entire team at Happy State Bank, thank you for not only sharing, but for bringing me in and making me feel like a part of your family.

To Pat, thank you for having the faith in me to tell the Happy State Bank story. I greatly value our friendship.

CONTENTS

FOREWORD

The only thing that bothers me is Kryptonite. I've never been scared of the dark. I cry when my grandbabies are born.

I just finished reading Sam's first manuscript of the book, and it makes me sound like a cross between Superman, George Washington, Martin Luther King, Jr., and (fill in the blank with the name of the person you most admire).

The truth is that I cuss, drink, and smoke too much. My ego is bigger than any building that I would ever want to "leap in a single bound." I've yelled at my wife and kids, and I've disappointed my parents and friends several times in their lives. And my coworkers can tell you of several of my screw-ups. But, we Christians will use the truthful saying that "I'm a sinner, saved by grace." And by the way, I do cry when my grandbabies are born.

I get to lead a really neat company—The Happy State Bank and Trust Co.—headquartered (on paper anyway) out of Happy, Texas—"The Town Without a Frown"—population 700 or so people in the middle of the Texas Panhandle.

Several people have expressed an interest in writing a book about the success of our bank—and when I first met Sam and read his book, *No More Excuses*, I loved his writing style. I thought we "hit it off" the first time I met him. And, as we discussed the possibilities of putting this book together, I finally found the courage to bring up a rather sensitive subject regarding its content. I told Sam that he could not write the book if he left out Jesus Christ. You see, I/we have depended on Him since before we purchased the bank. And, not that I would stereotype anyone, but from some of the things that Sam spoke of to me—and because of Sam's last name—it kind of hinted to me that maybe Sam didn't know Jesus the same way I did.

Sam wasn't offended when I asked, and we both agreed that we would think about it for a few weeks before we decided to proceed. My wife, Nancy, and I prayed about it. I discussed it with my bank board of directors. I asked Christian friends their opinions. And God gave me no "lightning bolt revelation," or even a minor nudge, of why Sam could or could not write the story of our bank's success. Sam called me about two weeks later and he told me that he, too, had discussed it with his wife, Renee, and thought through it. He thought that it would be a good book for other businesses to read because he would make our story, including Jesus, "more objective," because he was not a Christian. It did then, and does now, still sound good and reasonable to me.

Sam has told our story well. There are a few details that he left out, and he may have embellished a couple of small items—and the folks who have invested in, work at, or bank with Happy State Bank will tell you that he's nailed it—but I do need to clarify some things. You might say that I won't negotiate on these clarifications. It's just the way I see them because I know Jesus.

1) Sam refers to it as "non-negotiable" based on a "belief system." These are his terminologies for Happy State Bank's principles of business. Quite simply, we know, through God's Word—the Holy Bible—and through experience that some things are absolute truths.

I think the first absolute or non-negotiable formulated within the bank was the "Family First" principle. Before I worked here, I worked for several companies who claimed to have that principle, but didn't always follow through with it in a crunch. Therefore, I was determined that Happy State Bank would always place your family at the top. All the time. Every time. Period. I like the people I work with, and I've come to love several of them.

But I absolutely love my family. This is universal. Everyone loves their family. At least you should. And we're going to help you. If you miss a family event because you're working, you're fired… because your priorities suck (by the way, we've never had to fire anyone over this one).

As Sam points out, there will be times that I call in a marker. I may need you to work on a weekend or late at night—that's just part of working (or the curse, as Christians call it). There are trade-offs, but 99 out of 100 times, your family is going to be put first. My point is that putting your family first appears to me/us to be a godly principle, an absolute—OK, call it a non-negotiable.

My/our principles and absolutes are not just things we sincerely think should happen. We believe that this is the way God would want us to run this business. We know that it's bigger than Happy State Bank—certainly bigger than me.

I hope my "belief system" doesn't offend you. I hope you respect me for my convictions. I won't apologize. It's who I am and we are.

2) I have to respectfully disagree with Sam on one point. Toward the end of the book, Sam writes, "Remember, your belief system doesn't have to be based on any formal religious doctrine." I will assume that you are a grown-up business person if you are reading this book. So you can make up your own mind. I do *absolutely agree with him that you* need to figure out what *your* belief system entails and what *your* personal absolutes are. And *you* are responsible for *your* beliefs. To coin one of my favorite book titles: *No More Excuses.*

3) We're not "there" yet. Happy State Bank is not perfect. We have employees quit who think they were not given a fair shake. We have customers leave us because they don't like our service. I spend 60 percent of my time fixing problems.

Don't get me wrong. I still love my job and (most of the time) love going to the office. But we're always looking for ways to improve and get better. It drives me crazy to have a disgruntled employee or customer. I really hate having upset bank directors—they're the folks who can replace me in a moment's notice. I deal with those issues every day. But by using the principles—the non-negotiables in this book—the problems really are pretty rare. Still, everything we do is on trial every day, hoping that we'll keep improving.

4) I never expected this to be a Christian book. It's a business book that happens to be about a bank that has a Christian CEO and tries to operate under Christian principles. Not only Christians love their families or run good businesses. I know of more successful businesses run by non-Christians than I do by Christians. Unfortunately, I know of many businesses that claim to be Christian that operate in a, shall I say, un-Christlike fashion, and it makes me sick at my stomach. (But then, you know, I'm not naïve enough to think that we don't violate one of our absolutes every now and then as well. I will say that if it comes to our attention, we'll do everything in our power to attempt to fix it.)

I have never asked someone to bank with me because I'm a Christian, and I never will. I want people to bank with me because I run a dang good bank. Our service is awesome. We try to run a fair, honest, professional, and profitable company—and I get to lead it, and I just happen to be a Christian.

My non-negotiable to Sam was that having Christ in our bank had to be part of the story. My personal non-negotiable, absolute principle is also the reason for my being: To know Christ and to make Him known.

5) My name is in here way too much. My board of directors has been with me from day one. We've never started a board meeting without a prayer for guidance and wisdom. A couple of times I started into the business without a prayer and was quickly interrupted to back up and seek God's direction before proceeding.

Our bank officers and employees are consummate professionals who work hard every day, and they have held me accountable. On more than a few occasions, I've suggested that we proceed down a certain path, only to be told that there is a more honest way to go forward, or at least we should take time to pray about our next step before making the final decision.

I am surrounded by a phenomenal group of people. I get to be a player-coach. I get to be the point guard and/or quarterback, depending on your favorite sport. But let me assure you that I am just one cog in the machine. There's no false pride here. I know that the CEO is the big cog. It starts at the top. We've all heard those sayings. But this book gives me way more credit than it should, and not near enough is written about our board members, our officers and employees, and so many others who have held my hand through this marvelous journey.

Good Christian friends and prayer partners have girded me through good and not-so-good times. I've sought counsel from folks whom I knew had a love for Christ, and I could not have made it without their wisdom and advice.

And then there's my family. My bride (of 37 years), Nancy, holds me *so* accountable—and even though she's never spent a day working in an office, her counsel is always right on. I listened to a series by Christian financial counselor Larry Burkett 35 years ago and the only thing I remember from the lectures is this: Only have two business partners in life—your God and your spouse—and listen to both of them. Twice I've gone against advice from my wife, and it cost me both times. She is my perfect life mate and I am so blessed that we get to live life together.

And anytime I start getting a little cocky, my children bring me back to reality. They're out of the house now and doing well: J. Brad (and Heidi—and Jack, Sophie, and Baron), J. Grant (and Jenna—and Jarah and Gray), Tara (and Mark), and Crista. Wow, they have kept me up to date with what's going on in the world, what goes wrong at Happy State Bank, and how we (the bank—and me, as a person) can do better than we're doing now.

So to recap, just to clarify, our belief system is belief in Jesus Christ. We're good, but we're not perfect, and we're trying to get better. This is a good business book. And while you have to have good leadership at the top, you better surround yourself with, and listen to, good people.

Thanks and God bless,

—J. PAT HICKMAN
Chairman and CEO, Happy State Bank and Trust Co.

And some acknowledgments:

Thank you: Harold, Jim, Jack, Herbert, John, Dick, Herman, Richard, Linda, Brian, Carl, Harrell, Tom, Mike, Brian, Perry, Trent, C.W., George, Bailey, Rocky, Dale, Al, Drayton, DIII, Super Dave, Gary, Ross, Connie, Greg, Debbie, Kayla, Kurt, Willis, Doak, Rick, Alvia, Dianne, Renee, Steve, David, Missy, Beverly, Bud, Cindy, Glinda, Charlie, Corky, David, Gary, Jim, Mike, Brad, Steven, Marvin, Chris, Jim, Kim, and Micki. Sharon and Sam, too.

PREFACE

Two years have passed since I first met Pat Hickman, and I finally understand the value of what Pat has implemented in his bank. He has used his *belief system*, the fact that he *values people*, what is in his *control*, his *mission*, and his *non-negotiables* to demonstrate the message of accountability—the message I presented in my last book, *No More Excuses*. His leadership at Happy State Bank is a master's class in accountability.

Happy State Bank's story—and Pat's story—demonstrates the true value of identifying what is non-negotiable. From my many meetings with Pat and his team, I saw that if we accept specific accountability to others based on a deeply personal application of our own non-negotiables, then we can totally obsolete traditional leadership training, customer service training, and team building. That's powerful! And time-saving!

Non-negotiables transform everything and everyone they touch for the better. What follows on the pages of this book is what happened to Pat personally, what happens every day at Happy State Bank, what continues to happen to me...and what can happen in your life and your business—*if* you are willing to identify and take a stand for what is *non-negotiable* in your life.

Pat's example reminded me that our *actions* around accountability must expand if we are going to expand our Accountability Zone™. That's why I wrote this book—to expand the actions you are willing to take around accountability and inspire you as Pat inspired me.

—Sam Silverstein

PART ONE

A MAN ON A MISSION

1

HOW I MET PAT HICKMAN

A couple of years back, I had just finished speaking to a leadership group in Amarillo, Texas when I found myself upstaged.

That doesn't happen very often at events where I am the main speaker, and when it does I want to find out why it happens—so I can raise my game.

My topic that day had been *accountability,* my favorite subject. It's so much so that I wrote a book, *No More Excuses,* which is really my life's message. So when I speak, I am passionate, convinced, and committed to the accountability strategies I believe transform lives and organizations.

As I walked away from the podium that day in Amarillo, the crowd applauded enthusiastically. *That's a good sign,* I thought to myself, because these were people I wanted to do business with. Sharon Miner—a community leader in Amarillo who I later asked to come on board and become my director of operations— had organized this opportunity, and that was the whole reason I was here: to create new business ventures.

When I took my seat, though, another man strode forward, and when he stepped onto the stage, something happened in that room. The moment he took his position in front of the microphone, the whole ambience changed.

His name, he said, was J. Pat Hickman, and he was the CEO of Happy State Bank. Just hearing the unlikely name of his outfit, Happy State Bank, told me something was going to be different.

A PRESENCE AS BIG AS TEXAS

Pat wore a big pair of cowboy boots. In fact, I remember thinking that absolutely everything about him was big. He filled every single inch of that room, not just because he's a tall man, but because of his large presence and his sense of a serious personal goal. From the very first words he spoke, everyone in that room, including me, could sense that he was here for a reason. A big reason. A reason you wanted to know more about.

Within seconds, Pat had won over everyone, and I do mean everyone, who was in that room. Sharon saw it. I saw it.

As a professional speaker myself—and a past president of the National Speakers Association (NSA®)—I've been watching speakers long enough to know when someone has the audience on his or her side. This audience was definitely on Pat's side, but that wasn't all that had happened. In just a few minutes, he had them totally committed to his agenda. I remember looking around the room of standing, cheering people, and thinking that every single one of these people looked ready to open an account at Happy State Bank, apply to work there, or both! It was as though everything had become possible, for Pat and for everybody else, in just a matter of minutes.

> **Accountability is my favorite subject—so much so that I wrote a book, *No More Excuses*, which is really my life's message. So when I speak, I am passionate, convinced, and committed to the accountability strategies I believe transform lives and organizations.**

That flat-out astonished me. Who was this guy? Was he for real? How in the world had he done that? What were we all cheering for?

Something about what Pat Hickman had done was jaw-dropping all right, but I couldn't quite figure out what it was. I remember thinking at the time that he was either the genuine article, of a kind I had never encountered…or maybe, just maybe, the greatest con man west of the Mississippi.

PAT HAD ANSWERS

It's a little bit embarrassing to me now to own up that I wasn't quite sure which of those people I was looking at on the first day I encountered Pat Hickman. I do know I felt equal parts astonishment and skepticism as I watched Pat speak that day. Maybe I leaned more toward the skepticism. Maybe that's just how I am with new people who seem to have all the big answers to all the big questions. Maybe, at times, I wasn't sure anyone had answers to *any* of the big questions. And maybe I was sure no one could really be as "on"—at least not all the time—as Pat seemed to be during that speech. So yes, I suppose I was happy to assume that this guy was just a little too good to be true.

As it turned out, I was wrong about that. Very wrong.

Pat spent a lot of time that day talking about the mission of his organization: "Work hard, have fun, make money, while providing outstanding customer service and honoring the Golden Rule."

Something about the way he said that made me sit up and take notice.

Pat's words rushed over me like a waterfall during that speech. I remember that he also talked a lot about his employees. He told us where Happy State Bank's unique name came from, what its customer service standards were, and how the people who worked at the bank did their best to live up to that name and those standards. He shared how his people flat-out loved working at that bank, and how he loved working there, too. He was not ashamed to discuss his personal faith in Jesus Christ with anyone, and how that was the success of his bank. Take the time right now to reread his foreword and you'll see exactly what I mean. I especially remember him talking about his "absolutes"—the standards, the non-negotiables—he and his bank set in place that were not open to debate.

He talked about all of that—his belief system, his bank's mission, their non-negotiables—in a straightforward, compelling way. He talked about it all in much greater depth in my subsequent interviews with him—interviews I will share with you as this story unfolds. The main thing you need to know now, though, is what I took away on that very first day. It was a curiosity combined with a sense of skepticism I have already shared with you, the sense that this man was not, could not possibly be, for real.

I couldn't get it off my mind. How could a business leader in any industry, much less the banking industry, spend 20 minutes talking about the Golden Rule—and inspire a room full of skeptical people? What made him so special? Why him?

There had to be a catch somewhere.

The worst part was that I was a little afraid I had fallen under Pat's spell. Every once in a while, I caught myself thinking that I, too, wanted to work with this guy.

Why?

Was I growing soft?

Now I wanted to figure out who this man really was. During a break, I introduced myself to Pat and made a little small talk. I didn't get much time to size him up. I had to head off to another meeting Sharon had scheduled, so I made a mental note to research Pat and his bank after I made it back home to St. Louis. I wanted to call him.

I promised myself, though: There will be no giving in to the notion about *me* jumping on his bandwagon. I already had a bandwagon—accountability. Pat and his happy bank were a prospective client at that point. An interesting prospect. A prospect I was a little curious about. But nothing more. Or so I told myself as I left the hall.

Surprisingly, though, Pat and I were to meet much sooner than I expected.

HE WAS A MAN WITH A PURPOSE

Sharon had set up a luncheon the following day inviting leaders from the community to come hear about the accountability movement I steer. There were 15 people present including Pat Hickman.

I greeted Pat and cautiously talked with him before we sat down to our round-table session. I kept waiting for some kind of sign that he was faking it. It never came. Everything still seemed possible. He still was a man with a purpose.

What was this guy's game? I still hadn't figured him out.

HE READ MY BOOK

A month later, I was preparing to go back to Amarillo. I was scheduled to meet the general manager of a local network television affiliate station, the president of the Amarillo-Canyon business incubator, and even the mayor of Amarillo. (Canyon is a nearby town that's home to West Texas A&M University and an integral partner in the success of the Panhandle community.)

A thought passed through my mind: *As long as I'm in Amarillo....*

I asked Sharon whether, on this visit, we could stop by Happy State Bank and visit Pat Hickman.

Pat was still a prospect, I told myself. Just a prospect. Nothing more. Yet somehow, this was the meeting I was most looking forward to.

Sharon and I showed up for the meeting with Pat a few minutes early. He came out of his office to greet us and showed us in personally. His personality and charisma were just as big as I remembered. Within seconds, it somehow felt like we had been friends for a very long time.

As we settled in, Pat pointed to a copy of my book on accountability, *No More Excuses,* which was displayed prominently on his desk.

Pat said, "Your book has been on my desk longer than any other book. It's not because I haven't read it. It's because I've been showing it to everyone who walks in the room!"

We chatted for a while. I learned more about Pat and his bank. Then all of a sudden the conversation changed direction. Pat stood up from the sitting area, went to his desk, and printed off four sheets of paper. He handed them to me and said, "I want you to know what we believe. This is our unofficial values document. It's our list of 'absolutes.' It goes much deeper than what you see on these pages, though."

I read that list of values over several times and felt something shifting inside of me. It was as if he had just handed me 20 diamonds. It was their list of 20 absolutes. Their list of 20 values they did not deviate on. It was *No More Excuses* in action!

I asked Pat whether the commitments were listed in their order of importance. I guess maybe I was looking for a loophole. He shook his head, "No."

"They're all important," he said. "No one value on the list is more or less important than any other. This is how we do business."

Those 20 diamonds—those 20 absolutes—inspired this book and the title. I saw that list as Happy State Bank's non-negotiables—and I believe everyone and every organization needs their own non-negotiables.

Each and every one of Happy State Bank's Non-Negotiable Core Values™ was totally consistent with the bank's mission: *Work hard, have fun, make money, while providing outstanding customer service and honoring the Golden Rule.*

Not only that, each and every one of Happy State Bank's Non-Negotiable Core Values was totally consistent with Pat's personal belief system.

HE WANTED ME TO WRITE
THEIR HAPPY STORY

Without even meaning to, I had opened the door to the secret vault that held what made both Pat and the bank tick—and clearly demonstrates my message of accountability. Just by interacting with him, I could tell that Pat had fully committed to each of these non-negotiables personally—even though he called them by a different name.

While I felt honored that he would share his list of core values with me, I was still skeptical for some reason. I still wondered if anyone could really be as authentic as Pat seemed to be, and I questioned if anyone could actually consistently stick to these principles. There are lots of companies with words on a piece of paper.

Fine. This was what Pat was willing to commit to. I could accept the idea that this was how he personally did business—or wanted to. Did that mean every single person in the organization really bought in to all 20 of these values? The entire Happy State Bank culture was built around them? Was that even possible? Somehow, this still wasn't making sense to me.

TIME TO WRITE *NON-NEGOTIABLE*

Just as that thought flashed across my mind, though, Pat said, "This may sound like a crazy question, Sam, but I am going to ask it anyway. I have had several people ask to write a book about our bank, but it's never felt right. Is there any chance *you* might be interested in writing that book?"

I hadn't expected that one.

Pat went on: "People are always telling me there should be a book that tells our story, but I never have found the right person. I think it ought to be you."

Pat and I talked the idea over, and before I left the room I agreed to give the matter some thought and get back to him.

I told him I was interested, and that I would let him know my decision once I made it back to my office in St. Louis.

But on my way out of Amarillo, I questioned the fit. I thought it all over, and I found lots more reasons *not* to go forward with the book project than reasons to write it.

How much did I really know about this guy? All in all, I had only spent a couple of hours with him. What made this the right project for me? When had I ever written about another person or another business as the sole topic of a book? What profit could I make on such a deal? How would that profit compare to something else I might be doing with my time? I admit it. I was looking at the dollars first.

When I got back to St. Louis, I put together an elaborate proposal based on a similar project an author friend of mine had completed for a big company. It was a substantial deal. It covered all sorts of costs, marketing fees, and production expenses. When we had our next meeting and I presented the proposal to Pat. There was an obvious pause.

Pat said, "There is no way I can go to my board with a six-figure proposal." It just didn't work for Pat. Pat's a banker, not a publisher. He didn't want to proceed. We decided to let things lie.

Several weeks passed and I called Sharon. She said, "Sam, I've been thinking about that proposal."

I said, "I have too." I went over all my misgivings with her. I value her opinion and I needed it. We talked about how Pat didn't want to proceed with our proposal. I finally said to Sharon, "He just doesn't get the book business I guess."

That was just an excuse. In fact, this wasn't about Pat at all at this point. I was the one who wasn't getting it. As I told Sharon that I was about to tell Pat I didn't think the book project was a good fit, my explanation ended with the rhetorical musing, "Why me?"

There was a long silence.

Eventually I had to check to see whether or not Sharon was still on the line. She was.

"I'll tell you why it should be you, Sam," she said. "I watched you when Pat talked at the leadership event in Amarillo. I watched you at the round table. And I watched you during the meeting we had with Pat at the bank. Something about you changes when Pat's in the room. You think about what is possible in a different way. You have a different way of looking at your own purpose. He's got an important story to tell. And you need to hear it, too. I am telling you, Sam, if you walk away from this project, you will regret it. And if you ask me, you were born to do this book."

Now the silence was on my end of the line. I knew Sharon was right. I knew, in my heart, that I was meant to tell this story. It was an expansion of teaching accountability. It was an expansion of *No More Excuses*.

"Pat has spoken on several occasions of providence in his life. If providence is present in Pat's life, and if it brought the two of us together, then it must be present in my life, too," I admitted. Not only did I say that, but also I felt it in my heart! A few months earlier I might have struggled to say that, but the events happening in my life were affecting me, and in a good way. The door was open and I needed to walk through it. I just needed to say, "Yes."

"You're right, Sharon," I said. "I gotta run. Bye."

I had practically hung up on Sharon, but now it was clear as day what I needed to do and I didn't want to waste a minute. I called Pat and asked him, "Are you still interested in me writing that book?"

He responded, "Yes I am."

"Well, we are going to find a way to do this. Forget the agreement. Forget the cost. I'll write the book. We'll figure out who will publish it and how all the pieces go together as we proceed." I moved forward at that moment with great calmness, because inside I recognized what I really believed and I knew this was what I was supposed to do. Period!

2

THE BIRTH OF PAT'S FIRST
NON-NEGOTIABLE

Pat often describes himself as the "poster child for the American dream." As you will see, there is a lot of truth to that description. How does someone who never graduated from college, who had a net worth of only $8,000, come to be the CEO and a major stockholder of a bank?

How can someone buy a bank in 1990—with only $10 million in assets and one location—and build that little bank into 35 locations with an excess of $2.5 billion in assets?

How does an organization year after year turn a more-than-healthy profit—even when there was a crisis in 2008 in their industry and the economy faced its worst performance in 70 years?

The answer, I learned, lies in the non-negotiables Pat and his leadership team created for himself and for his business. For example, "Doing what's right" is one primary non-negotiable for Pat. It's also the first of the five accountabilities I teach in *No More Excuses.*

Pat believes that once he gives his word on something, he will not consciously choose to go against that word because keeping your word with someone is what is right. It's an absolute for him. It's a personal standard that extends into every aspect of everything he does. It's something he operates and lives by, 24/7, no matter what. It's what he values.

But it wasn't always like that.

Pat is human like the rest of us. He had to *work his way up* to that point where doing what's right was not just an opinion, not just a belief, but a non-negotiable component of who he really is as an individual. It's something he controls.

Very early on in this project, I had the privilege of hearing how Pat turned his own *opinions and actions* about doing what's right into a *non-negotiable*. Here, in Pat's own words, is the true story of how he and his investors bought Happy State Bank, which offers a great lesson in this process.

> Carl Small owned a majority share in the bank we wanted to buy, which was located in Happy, Texas. Carl was meeting regularly with me about the possibility of me buying the bank. We were discussing all kinds of issues for two or three months. He knew I wanted to lead the group that bought his bank, and he knew what kind of bank I wanted to run, and he knew I was out raising money.
>
> Weeks went by. Months went by. Carl and I were getting more and more excited. I finally figured I had enough investors put together to pull this off. We were at a little under a million bucks. Carl owned just under 61 percent of the bank. We had to buy his share, but we couldn't stop there. We knew that, in order to have control, we had to own 67 percent of the bank. Ideally, we wanted to buy out all the stockholders. We just didn't know yet if we could do that or not.
>
> So the first goal was just to buy Carl out. The second goal was to buy our way up to 67 percent. And the third goal was to buy out everybody.
>
> Now, through all of these meetings, Carl and I had never talked about what price we wanted. We had

talked about everything else under the sun, but he hadn't even hinted about how much money was supposed to go his way for selling us his shares in the bank. Looking back on it, it seems kind of crazy, but that's what happened.

Now, at the time, I was working as manager of the Canyon, Texas branch of First National Bank of Amarillo. Throughout this whole period, I told my boss exactly what I was doing. I didn't want him to hear about it through a rumor. That would've been horrible. So I was very heads-up with him. I told him, "Hey, I'm trying to buy a bank, but please don't fire me. My wife's expecting our fourth kid. I can't stand to be without a job."

And eventually there came a point where my boss said to me, "Hickman, you've got five weeks to figure out whether this is happening or not."

Five weeks was a very narrow window, given the complexity of what we were doing. It just seemed like no time at all to wrap this thing up. But I said to myself, well, those are the cards I got dealt. Let's go ahead and play them.

Time passed faster than I wanted it to. Weeks went by. I realized it was about time for me to talk pricing with Carl. My investors said to me, "OK, for Carl's 60.5 percent, you can pay $750,000. You're on your own. Go make it happen." That was as high as I could go.

The way it played out, Carl and I scheduled a meeting to nail down the numbers, to figure out whether or not this thing was going to happen. And remember, I was running out of time. In fact, the next day, I had to let my boss know yea or nay, was I in or not.

I don't know if anybody ever tried to buy a bank before at the McDonald's located at 34th and Coulter in Amarillo, Texas, but that's where we met to try to seal the deal. We went through all the pleasantries. We talked around the subject for little bit, and then finally I just said, "Carl, I've never bought a bank before, and I don't know where to start."

And he said, "Well, I've never sold one before."

I said, "Carl, give me a hint, let me know what we're looking at."

"Well," he answered, "I'll tell you. My wife and I talked this over. We want a million dollars. That's our price."

And I just looked at him.

I said, "Carl, I'm not gonna insult you. I think my number is so low, you're not going to want to hear it. And I don't want to do that. We're so far apart. Let's just shake hands say we gave it the old college try, and then when we leave this McDonald's, we can leave as friends. This is not going to work."

And I meant it. It really wasn't any negotiating ploy. I just couldn't bear looking him in the eye and tell him I only had $750,000 to work with.

So that's where we left it. Carl said he understood. I didn't even make a counteroffer. We spent the next hour and a half talking, sincerely, about how good it could've been if we had been able to put that deal together. But at that point, we had both concluded it wasn't going to happen.

We left the McDonald's. I called my investors and told them the deal had fallen through. Then I went home and cried like a baby. And I am not exaggerating about that. The only time in my whole life that I cried harder than I cried that night was the night that my dad passed away.

That whole night was just plain horrible. My wife and I prayed for strength. I was lucky to have somebody like Nancy by my side to pray with. I remember feeling that everything I had experienced in my life had prepared me for the opportunity of buying that bank. I remember feeling, deep down in my heart, that this was what I was supposed to be doing. I remember having to step back and say to myself, "Well, you either trust God or you don't." So, with my wife's help, I decided I trusted Him. It was time to move on to whatever He had planned next for me.

The next morning, I went to work, I told my boss that the deal had fallen through. He tried to give me all kinds of supportive talk about how this was the best thing for me, and how I'd be bored stiff trying to run a little bank like that, and how I was the heir apparent at the bank I was working at. A whole bunch of stuff like that. But in my heart, I still felt just terrible.

Later that day, I talked again with one of the investors. He could tell I was shaken up. He told me, "Pat, I've made a lot of deals in my life. You can relax about this. It may not be today, maybe not tomorrow, but someday soon, three days, three months, three years, Carl's gonna call you back. You just be patient."

I told him I wished that I felt that way, but I just didn't.

Friday passed. It was a horrible weekend, and I was really depressed, but I got through it. Monday morning, I went back to work, and about 9:30 in the morning, my secretary came in and told me, "Carl's on the phone for you."

I picked up the phone, said, "Hello." I heard the first words out of Carl's mouth to me since we had parted company at that McDonald's: "You little so-and-so. I didn't sleep good all weekend, and I hope you didn't, either."

I laughed and said, "Well, Carl, I just can't tell you how heartbroken I am that we couldn't get this together."

Then, without any transition at all, he just said, "Tell them six-fifty. That's my bottom line."

I could hardly believe my ears. I said, "Are you serious?"

He said, "Yes, I'm serious. That's all we can go, but we'll take six-fifty."

I said, "Carl, I called all my investors and told them that the deal was off. I guess I'm about to call them all back to make sure they're good to go with this. But assuming they are, Carl, I think you just sold a bank."

Of course, my face was beaming as I made those calls. As it turned out, everybody who had been in told me that they would stay in. That seemed like the end of the story. But it wasn't.

I called my boss. I told him, "I wasn't lying to you on Friday. I wasn't trying to buy time, honest. I just got a call from Carl. The deal is back on. I'm giving you two weeks' notice."

He said he understood.

Then I set up a meeting and got all my investors together, and the strangest thing happened. One of them looked me in the eye and said, "Hickman, you gave up too easy."

I said, "What do you mean?"

He said, "Well, if he dropped that much after one conversation, that means he would've dropped more than that if you'd asked him to. You can probably get this deal done for $600,000. You have to try for that."

I just stared at him. He actually wanted me to go back and try to get a lower price...after I had personally agreed to a figure that was less than what my board of directors had said was my maximum!

I said, "You don't understand. I made an agreement with the man."

He didn't care. This one investor kept insisting I had to try to renegotiate the deal. He was loud, he was boisterous, he was insistent. I won't tell you his name. All I will tell you is that he wanted a better price, even though I had given my word to Carl. And the rest of the investors agreed with him.

I want you to look very carefully at what happens next. At this point, Pat did not yet have a non-negotiable. He didn't have a consistent standard he was willing to fight for. Instead, he had an opinion that he ought to do what's right if it's at all possible to do so—and a record of action that showed he did that most times. That's what most of us have, but not what most of us need.

I said, "Guys, guys you're killing me here. Listen, I work for you. If that's what you tell me to do, I'll go back there, and I will try to renegotiate this. But I have to tell you, this is not a good thing you're asking me to do."

They told me to do it anyway. So I said I would.

I left that meeting, I spent a little time working on my courage, I picked up the phone, and I called Carl.

We traded hellos and such, and then I said, "Carl, I want to renegotiate the price."

There was a little pause. He said, "What do you mean?"

"Well," I said, feeling more than a little shaky, "I talked to my investors, and we want to get it for 600."

There was a change in his voice that I had never heard before, and haven't heard since. Carl's tone was suddenly icy. Over the phone, he told me, "Pat, that price just went up to 750. And if you try to negotiate, the deal is off."

Notice that Carl had a non-negotiable here! It was a very clear one for him, and it also might be described as: "Do what's right." Carl gave Pat the benefit of the doubt, based on a past relationship, but as a result of having that non-negotiable, Carl knew exactly what to do next: Make a final offer…and walk away if anyone tried to change it.

I took a deep breath. Then I said, "I don't blame you one bit, sir. We will pay the 750." And I meant it.

We said goodbye. And we hung up.

Now watch how Pat's opinions and actions about doing what's right turn into a non-negotiable about doing what's right. For Pat, and for all of us. It's the act of taking a stand that makes that transition possible.

I went back to my guys, and I said, "OK. Here's the deal. Here's how the conversation went. He heard what I wanted, he didn't like it, and he told me that the price is now 750. Not only that. He told me that if I were to try to negotiate on the price at all, the whole deal was out the window. I have given the man my word we are going to pay $750,000 for his share in this bank, and by damn, that's what we're going to pay for it. If that costs me your support, so be it. You guys can get out if you want, but if you stay in, I need to say two things. First and foremost, one way or another, I am going to keep my word to Carl. Second, please don't ever ask me to go back on my word like that again. I cannot, I will not do that, ever again."

Pat has drawn a line in the sand. He is living a non-negotiable.

> None of the investors gave me any static. We bought the bank for $750,000. Now, I realize that $100,000 may sound like a lot of money, and that some people might say we lost that $100,000. In fact, that was a very small price to pay for the lesson we all learned from that experience. We don't go back on our word.

Let's get very clear on what happened to Pat here, because it's the same thing that needs to happen to us as we create our own non-negotiables.

Initially, you will recall, Pat had only opinions and actions when it came to doing what's right. Then he agreed to go back and ask Carl for more money, even though he and Carl had already come to terms. Pat knew in his heart that wasn't right.

Today, he knows that he should have told his investors: "You know what? I told the man I was going to buy his share of the bank for $650,000. I can't go back to him and ask for more. It's not right. If that number doesn't work for you, then we just shouldn't buy the bank. This is what I agreed to. And I'm not budging."

He should have done that, back when he was in negotiations with Carl. But he didn't. Today, he would.

He has a personal non-negotiable now: *"I do what's right."* That non-negotiable lines up with his *belief system*—that he values people and knows what he can control—and his mission, which I'll tell you more about in the following chapters.

It cost Pat Hickman $100,000 to finalize that standard. But if you ask him, he will tell you that it was the best $100,000 ever spent—not only for him, but also for the whole bank, and indeed everyone in his life. Now Pat knows exactly what the non-negotiable is. He is now in control of this aspect of his life.

That means his relationships now have guidelines everyone understands and can agree on. Without those kinds of guidelines, life doesn't work as well as it should!

3

THE POSITIVE POWER OF A NON-NEGOTIABLE

If you're dieting right now, congratulations! You're in good company. At any given time, 50 percent of the American population is on a diet. One of the first recorded "diet plans" was in 1558 by an Italian businessman who had become so large, his doctors had given up. This man created a diet of just 12 ounces of food per day plus 14 ounces of wine. He lost weight, spread the news, and it became popular.

Over the next few hundred years, there were many more inventive plans created to lose weight. In 1820, Lord Byron, an English poet, popularized the vinegar and water diet, which entailed drinking water mixed with apple cider vinegar. In 1925, the Lucky Strike cigarette brand launched the "Reach for a Lucky instead of a sweet" campaign, capitalizing on nicotine's appetite-suppressing superpowers.

From the '30s grapefruit diet to the '50s cabbage soup diet, from the '60s introduction of Weight Watchers® to the '80s Jazzercise® craze, from cleansing to stuffing yourself with meat, diets are all about two things—losing weight, of course, and mastering control.

Diets either control your portions for you—from selected food groups—or teach you how to control your portions. Many provide "guidelines" that tell you what to order at popular restaurants or what should comprise your grocery list.

The control they teach in order to help you lose weight is really all about making a list of dietary "non-negotiables"—only we all know most of us don't keep these for life! If we did, 50 percent of us would have eventually learned to eat right—and be smaller!

This is not a diet book, and I'm not a nutritionist, but here's the point: If I know ahead of time my dietary non-negotiables before I go into a restaurant, I will be in control—and order the best healthy choice, not my favorite weight-gaining choice. Dietary non-negotiables free me to achieve my weight-loss goals and keep me—and my appetite—in control.

In the same way, if I know my life or company non-negotiables, they free me to achieve personal or corporate goals. They give me control—the positive power of a non-negotiable.

When we know what in our life is non-negotiable, we know where our power and control really lie—and everyone wants the freedom of control.

Whether you realize it or not, if you don't know your non-negotiables you are probably not reaching your potential. If you don't know what your non-negotiables are, you probably don't know why you're not living the life you should be living or achieving at the level you could be achieving or having the relationships you could be having. That's because you don't know where you really stand. And neither does anyone else.

At the foundational level, establishing a non-negotiable is a choice to maintain control over a specific area in your life.

We choose to give up control all the time—health, finances, emotions, happiness, relationships, you name it. What adjustments can you make in your life to reclaim your control in these areas where you have talked yourself into believing that you're not in control? Because you can't have a non-negotiable for something you don't believe you can control.

YOU CAN REGAIN CONTROL

Let me give you an example of what I mean. Several years ago when I owned a window and door manufacturing business, our delivery time was six to eight weeks—unacceptably long. The market wanted a high-quality product and they wanted it quickly. Consistently high-quality products, short turn-around times, and exemplary customer service had all become negotiable in our business. Should it have been a surprise that we were hemorrhaging money, that everything we owned was leveraged to secure our loans, and that we were on the brink of going out of business?

We didn't have a belief that consistent quality and service was critical. You could tell that by looking at our actions. We made excuses for why the windows had service problems and why the customers had to continuously wait for them. It wasn't until I was able to get the leadership team to sit down and say, "Quality and delivery times are non-negotiable. We will deliver a well-built product and do it in a week's time," that things changed for the better.

It only took six weeks' time from the day we made that decision to get all of our product cleaned up, all our manufacturing lines relaid to support the new direction, and to start fulfilling the promise to our customers that we would deliver their quality windows no later than one week after they ordered them.

Guess what? It wasn't very long after that our cash flow totally changed, our bottom line went from red to black, and we were able to pay off all of our loans.

If we want to, we can believe that we don't have control of situations, and we can create excuses or justifications—or we can get "fed up" and choose to establish a non-negotiable to fix something that is not working. It is entirely up to us whether we assume control.

Case in point: For years, I allowed our company to make excuses, deliver inconsistent quality, and take too long to get the windows and doors to our customers. I was wrong when I just went along with what we were doing. I was wrong when I accepted the status quo and let our debts continually rise. It flat-out wasn't true that we couldn't deliver a consistently great product in a short period of time. We could.

What inaccurate beliefs about your own business, or maybe your life, could you be protecting now? How could you change them? In what area of your life are you ready to resume full control?

> **People who build powerful, positive non-negotiables are not perfect, but they are more likely to have lives that function well and attract others!**

You have to know what you want to change from, in order to identify what you want to change to. Creating a non-negotiable is the very act of taking back control of an aspect of your life that is out of control.

The moments between being out of control and taking control can be incredibly hard. Those moments are full of risk, full of questioning if you're doing the right thing, because ultimately it's easier to relinquish control.

In 2006, actor Will Smith portrayed Chris Gardner, an over-the-top successful American entrepreneur, Wall Street legend, motivational speaker, author, and philanthropist—who struggled with homelessness off and on for about a year when his son was small. In the book and subsequent movie, *The Pursuit of Happyness,* Gardner does what he has to do, coping with failure but never letting himself quit. He fights to move forward and keep his dream for a better life by taking control of whatever it is at the moment he has control over. He waits in line for shelter and a meal, tries to sell portable bone-density scanners to local doctors for money, and applies for a stockbroker position after he impresses a manager for Dean Witter by solving a Rubik's Cube® while sharing a cab—each challenge demonstrating him continually taking responsibility for his life and his son's. He never gives up—despite the seeming hopelessness of his circumstances. *His belief that he could do better for himself and his son made all the difference—it's what he had control over.*

This is such a critical point. *Your beliefs are what you have control over first. And those beliefs lead to developing non-negotiables.*

Regardless of how much of a failure you may feel in some area of your life—or maybe all of it—you can move forward by taking control of what you really do have control over, starting with your beliefs. Then move on to what externally it is that you have control over and seize it. It's OK that you may have failed, but it's not OK to quit.

When a business takes control of what it has control over, it moves forward. You can talk about the economy for hours and all its effects on your business, but when the conversation is over, nothing will have changed. If you take control of what is really in your control, however, things really can begin to change.

I don't care how off-course you may be right now, or how off-course your company may be, non-negotiables—taking control of what you can about product design, services offered, or your sales effort, and making proactive decisions—can right any off-course area. Non-negotiables have the power to transform every part of your life and company where you begin to define them.

At the very least, once you know what your non-negotiables are, your relationships—all your relationships, not just your workplace relationships—will work better.

NON-NEGOTIABLES PRODUCE PERSONAL FREEDOM

At the end of the day, non-negotiables are all about assuming personal responsibility for, and control of, your own life. In fact, whether or not you are actually in control of any given aspect of your life is the big "gut check" of this whole process.

People who have no non-negotiables in their lives have effectively yielded control of their lives to other people or circumstances.

If someone consistently experiences road rage, for instance, that person may point to all kinds of external circumstances that supposedly "caused" the conflicts with other drivers. In reality, though, the situation is this: They didn't formulate and live a non-negotiable that connects to managing his or her own emotions on the road. As a result, that driver lost control of their emotions and behaviors. No non-negotiable equals no control.

Similarly, you probably heard a lot of senior executives making a lot of excuses justifying poor financial results in the period following the 2008-2009 financial crisis. These executives tried to lead themselves and others to believe that outside circumstances had more to do with their company's performance than anything happening inside the enterprise. In fact, the most important variable was interior. Any time you are tempted to fixate on outside circumstances rather than internal non-negotiables as the determining element of your performance, you have lost control. Losing control is customarily followed by one or more excuses explaining why you have no control...and that never looks good.

"If it weren't for the kind of childhood I experienced, I would have...."

"If it weren't for the problems I had in school, I would have...."

"If it weren't for the economy, I would have...."

No more excuses!

People who have no non-negotiables in their lives have effectively yielded control of their lives to other people or circumstances.

So, once a standard like "Do what's right" becomes a non-negotiable for you, you control each and every situation to which it applies.

When you have a personal non-negotiable, you're not relegating responsibility for the outcome of those situations to someone or something else, you don't make excuses, and you don't accept a lower standard. You know what the outcome is going to be: You do what's right.

As a result, you have created personal authority for what happens around all issues that connect to doing what's right. There's no longer any doubt, no confusion about what you should do, no reason to blame some external source for what happens. When it comes to doing what's right, it's all on you.

> **Your beliefs are what you have control over first. And those beliefs lead to developing non-negotiables.**

Once you make your way to the level of the non-negotiable, "Do what's right" isn't just something you hold as an opinion or something you do once in a while. It's an absolute, something you accept personal control over, every single time. It's an intrinsic part of who you are as an individual. It's non-negotiable, and it becomes a personal strength. You are now in control of this element of your life. No one else is!

Just like Pat did, you can identify, reinforce, and take a stand for your own beliefs, develop a mission—and develop them into non-negotiables. Of course, my aim is not to get you to take on the exact same non-negotiables that Pat has. (I will say, though, that "Do what's right" is one of my non-negotiables, and probably should be one of yours, too.) My aim is to help you identify and strengthen your own non-negotiables—whatever you determine them to be. That's how you determine who you really are as an individual—and as a company. People who build powerful, positive non-negotiables are not perfect, but they are more likely to have lives that function well and attract others!

I'm not afraid to tell people, "Look, if you're talking about service to others, or transparency, or family, or any other slogan, but your actions don't ever involve taking a stand at any time, or helping others to take a stand for them, then they aren't really *standards* in your life." That's how you can tell that you haven't yet adopted them as non-negotiables. You haven't yet taken a stand. You haven't yet drawn a line in your life and said, "You know what? I'm not going over that line"—and then taken action that matches those words. If what you say you believe isn't showing up in your life or your organization, then how can you say you believe it?

NON-NEGOTIABLES AFFECT
YOUR BOTTOM LINE

When Pat wanted to buy a bank, he didn't give up. He started with $8,000 and a dream. Did he experience a setback? Yes. But it birthed his first non-negotiable—evidence of him taking control of what he could to produce positive change. He knew what he truly believed, why he believed it, and what he wasn't willing to compromise.

Today, Pat's once-tiny bank is now one of the largest banks in the state of Texas. It has 35 locations and over $2.5 billion in assets. (Those numbers are growing all the time, and will certainly be out of date by the time you read this.) Every single one of those 35 branches is run exactly the way Pat ran that little branch in Canyon, Texas—with non-negotiables.

Even if you're not particularly interested in the world of banking, you may be interested to learn that Pat's bank has posted a 10-year annualized return to its investors of 13.35 percent, and has never had any problems issuing stock. That's pretty remarkable, considering the financial meltdown of 2008-2009, and the Great Recession that followed!

There came a point where I asked myself: "*What if you ran your life the way Pat ran his? What if you ran your company the way Pat ran his? What if you built your world around non-negotiables?"*

Pat is passionate. He's "all in"—and has been from the beginning. He wanted to own a bank more than anything else. He was driven by what he knew he was called to do. Pat's story of passion and innovation is not an isolated one—though his commitment to non-negotiables is remarkable. Like I mentioned earlier, Chris Gardner's passion to make it fueled his will and desire to control what he could—starting with what he believed—and change his future. Refusing to quit, to go at it again, drawing a line in the sand—adopting a non-negotiable attitude—was a game-changer for both of these innovative and determined leaders. Both Pat and Chris experienced the positive power of a non-negotiable.

NON-NEGOTIABLES FREE YOU TO HAVE REAL CONTROL

Pat Hickman embodies the reality of non-negotiables: When we know what in our life is non-negotiable, we know where our power and control really lie—and everyone wants the freedom of control. He demonstrates that when we know what is and isn't an option for us, that may just be the most freeing and empowering piece of information we will ever encounter.

Pat's life—and bank organization—show that when you do find your own non-negotiables, when you live them with all your might, they determine who you really are. The story of Carl Small illustrates this well. Through that encounter and experience, Pat defined a non-negotiable—and who he really was.

No matter your profession, background, education, or culture, what you are willing to take a stand for is what ultimately produces your greatest and most enduring contributions in life.

I have chosen to write this book, not only because Pat asked me to write the story of Happy State Bank, but also because I have found that most of us haven't clearly identified something we believe in deeply enough to take a stand for—and that means that most of us have not awakened our own power, either in our own lives or in the lives of our families, teams, and organizations.

My experience is that people usually don't really think much about what they believe—which is the starting point of defining a non-negotiable. They simply act the way they have always acted. They waver when their stated beliefs are put to the test. Most people mix and match—they are one person at home, another person at work, another person at their house of worship, and so on.

Just because you say you believe something doesn't make it truth. If your actions don't support the belief, then it really isn't a belief. It is essential to have a clear set of non-negotiables that can awaken your own unique, authentic personal power.

ALL FIVE MUST BE IN ALIGNMENT

Non-negotiables are fairly rare, both in our organizations and at the individual level. One reason is that most people and businesses haven't yet bothered to identify a coherent *belief system* or a coherent *mission*. Another reason is that even though people may think they have a belief system and a mission, these may not actually be in alignment with each other. They may even conflict. The result—inconsistency and contradictions. Very often, when someone says, "I refuse to compromise on such-and-such," reality proves just the opposite.

If you've ever heard someone say, for instance, *"Customer service is our top priority"* and then turn around and disrespect a customer, you know exactly what I'm talking about. Not long ago, I had this experience with a major air carrier, a company whose mission statement claimed to put the customer first, but whose employees apparently hadn't seen that standard carried out in real life. It wasn't even on their radar screen. They had no shared belief system that connected to the mission. They didn't focus on what they could actually control and they didn't understand what valuing people really means. They had no standard against which to measure putting the customer first. There was a disconnect. As a result, my problem not only didn't get resolved in a way that made me feel like I was their top priority, but also it made me wonder why the company bothered to even mention customers in the mission statement in the first place!

Here's the point: Non-negotiables don't happen just because of the noises we make with our mouths. There is an art to identifying them...and living by them. This book asks: What's *not* open to negotiation in your life...and how do you know?

Yes, there are times in our lives or our businesses when it makes sense to negotiate, to collaborate, to split the difference when we are trying to resolve divisive issues. Sometimes a stalemate only seems to bring all productivity to a halt—and compromise is essential to keep business moving. Sometimes, it's healthy to agree to disagree and revisit the discussion later when clear minds can initiate new ideas of resolution.

This book isn't about those kinds of times or events, though.

This book is about what's truly non-negotiable—and the story of a man and his bank who demonstrate how to live by them. Happy State Bank marketplace results prove it's critical to know what you believe. Its CEO is someone who knows exactly what his standard in life is, who knows what he believes in deeply enough to take a stand for it, who doesn't ever waver on what is non-negotiable in his life, and who is the same guy everywhere he goes—and the trickle-down effect in his organization is undeniable. The culture that inspires *accountability* that permeates Happy State Bank is a marvel of success. The level of accountability in which they operate is an outflow of their list of 20 non-negotiables.

This is what I teach everywhere I go and talk about Happy State Bank: The Power of Accountability™ is when you *value people, know what you believe, what your mission is, what is in your control, and what is truly non-negotiable for you, and everyone on your team understands and lives by those non-negotiables, then you will create an environment where people can be their very best both for themselves and the organization. The natural outflow is a place where accountability is abundant and people keep their commitments to themselves and to others.*

This definition clearly defines Happy State Bank and its leader. Pat is a great role model for business communities everywhere—and a great example of the positive power of control that non-negotiables afford. Happy State Bank is a great role model for any industry that wants a seamless culture from top to bottom.

FIVE COMPONENTS—ONE DIRECTION

To achieve the control that non-negotiables afford, you have to begin a process, a journey of development personally, as a team and as a company. But like all implemented principles, the ultimate success for you begins with you.

The process involves clearly identifying your beliefs, what you believe you really have control over, your mission, truly valuing people and then deciding what's non-negotiable in your life, and/or department or company. Whatever your level of leadership, this teaching and instruction in this book can transform your life—and the outflow of your life to the areas where you have influence.

Pat has lived this process. He has clearly identified his beliefs, mission, and absolutes—what I call non-negotiables.

Pat's *belief system* is his personal faith in Jesus Christ. You don't have to have his specific belief system in order to establish your own non-negotiables, but you do need to identify what you really are willing to live in *your* life. Your belief system might be a religious or spiritual tradition, or it might be something you learned from your parents or from someone else who was important to you in life. Alternatively, your belief system might come about from conclusions you have reached as an adult, after a long period of personal assessment and contemplation. Your belief system is the beginning of what you are willing to stand up for in life. You don't have to share it with others unless you want to, but you have to know *what you stand for* as a result of living these beliefs.

> The Power of Accountability™ is when you value people, know what you believe, what your mission is, what is in your control, and what is truly non-negotiable for you, and everyone on your team understands and lives by those non-negotiables, then you will create an environment where people can be their very best both for themselves and the organization. The natural outflow is a place where accountability is abundant and people keep their commitments to themselves and to others.

A lot of people ask me: "How do I know what my belief system is?" I'll look more closely at this issue in the next chapter, but here's the best short answer I've found:

Your belief system is the still, small voice inside your heart and head that helps you to pose, and answer, the question "What's the right thing to do here?" And by the way, that's a question I now ask myself constantly, as a direct result of having interviewed Pat so many times. I know I'm not the only one whose personal belief system has come into sharper focus as the result of knowing him.

Pat's focus on what he can *control* allows him to avoid the mental distractions of the world around him and focus on the task at hand. He knows that the first thing he has control over is what he believes. He knows that by making decisions around what he can control he gets results, not excuses. And he teaches the people around him to do the same. At Happy State Bank they simply do not accept excuses.

Pat *values people*. It is evident in almost every conversation. When someone asks about his or the bank's success he always credits the people around him. When he is in the bank or out to lunch or walking to his car he is always engaging people, praising people, and acknowledging people. Pat values people, loves people, and trusts people. Everyone around him knows that and they are inspired by it.

Pat's *mission* tells him exactly why he gets up in the morning: *Work hard, have fun, make money, while providing outstanding customer service and honoring the Golden Rule.* The officer team of the bank worked very hard to craft that mission. The bank's mission aligns with Pat's personal mission and the personal missions of the other officers at the bank.

Notice that Pat's mission aligns with his beliefs. Pat's beliefs do not change when he walks in the front door of his company or in the front door of his home. Neither does anything in his life that is non-negotiable. Your mission must clearly identify your purpose, your reason for existing—and it must align with your belief system.

> **Pat's mission tells him exactly why he gets up in the morning: Work hard, have fun, make money, while providing outstanding customer service and honoring the Golden Rule.**

Pat's *non-negotiables* establish the specific guidelines for behavior where upholding the non-negotiable is an absolute must—no ifs, ands, or buts! There are a lot more than 20 of these absolutes in Pat's life, but in this book our focus is on the 20 non-negotiables proliferated throughout his organization because they connect so powerfully to both Pat and to the organization he and his board of directors have built.

Pat *lives* these 20 non-negotiables day in and day out. He serves as the primary role model in *implementing* them (not just talking about them) on a daily basis. He has used them to build a life and a culture that is completely in harmony with both his belief system and his mission. They are *how* he "walks his talk." They are what allowed him to turn the American dream into a *reality* for himself, his customers, his stakeholders, and anyone else who is fortunate enough to have a relationship with Happy State Bank.

In the same way, your non-negotiables are the positive benchmarks that:

a) Line up perfectly with your beliefs and your mission.

b) Respect the rights of others.

c) Are not open to negotiation.

In the introduction to my book, *No More Excuses,* I said it this way: "When you are in the Accountability Zone™, your actions are fully in harmony with your promises to stakeholders. I call this alignment" (p. xiv).

A MASTER'S CLASS IN ACCOUNTABILITY

Two years have passed since I first met Pat Hickman, and I finally know what happened to me in Amarillo. Pat Hickman's demonstration of valuing people, his belief system, his mission, his focus on what was in his control, and his non-negotiables showed me the power of what I teach and the book I wrote—*No More Excuses*—and provided a master's class in accountability. Accountability is the natural outflow of non-negotiables.

I saw through Pat's example the true value of identifying what is non-negotiable, and that when we accept specific accountability to others based on a deep, personal application of our own non-negotiables, we can totally obsolete traditional leadership training, customer service training, and team building.

That is powerful!

Non-negotiables transform everything and everyone they touch for the better. I personally have come to define a non-negotiable this way:

A positive standard that respects the rights of others, and is absolute.

This definition has evolved over time and is a definition that expresses commitment and simultaneous respect and consideration of others. Non-negotiables are the foundation of the success of Happy State Bank. Non-negotiables are the foundation of my success as well.

We have to know, unequivocally, who we are, what we believe, and what we stand for. The result of this kind of self-awareness is the ability to identify what is non-negotiable for us—and then we must fully live those parts of our lives.

So, what in your life is non-negotiable? It might be the absolute "no way" position that a truly great professional athlete takes with regard to illegal performance-enhancing drugs. It might be the position someone takes with regard to their marriage and the sanctity of that relationship. Or, it might connect to a belief that we should treat all people as we ourselves would want to be treated. However it expresses itself, a non-negotiable is a line we draw in the sand—a line we don't try to blur. It's not something we say for show. It's something we live.

PART TWO

THE POWER OF ACCOUNTABILITY

4

Defining a Sound
Belief System

Defining your non-negotiables begins with building your foundation—your *belief system*. Your belief system is the bedrock on which your life is built—and the strength that will sustain it throughout your career and lifetime. Therefore, your foundation is critical. Just as in an actual brick and mortar building, if your foundation crumbles, so do you.

Consider the evolution of construction. People have constructed buildings and other structures since prehistory, including bridges, amphitheaters, dams, electrical transmission towers, roads, and canals. Building materials in present use have a long history and some of the structures built thousands of years ago can still be regarded as remarkable. The history of construction overlaps that of structural engineering, and there are structural marvels standing to this day—some even labeled "wonders of the world," such as the Great Pyramid of Giza. What the man-made wonders all have in common can loosely be identified as a right foundation.

Addressing construction and engineering flaws determines if a structure lasts or not. For example, when Lisa Halaby, who graduated from Princeton in 1974 with a B.S. in Architecture and Urban Planning, married King Hussein of Jordan in 1978 and became Queen Noor Al-Hussein, she adopted her new homeland of Jordan—and in the early years of her new position she identified challenges that could be improved. As she drove through its towns, she found crumbling buildings and unstable infrastructures. She had worked in the country years prior to her marriage on building projects associated with an airline. It had become apparent from that experience and her observations that it was critical for Jordan to have standardized building codes.

She writes in her memoir, *Leap of Faith, Memoirs of An Unexpected Life*, that not long after her marriage, she invited the Minister of Public Works to her office at Al Ma'Wa. She discovered he had access to books of standard building codes from countries all over the world, but Jordan did not have a binding one of their own.

With King Hussein's agreement, she called for a meeting of the key engineers and architects in Jordan to ask what problems they encountered and what they felt should be done to establish uniform building requirements. There was general agreement that the government and the private sector should work together to formulate such regulations.

Over the next few years, the Royal Scientific Society produced Jordan's first building code. Queen Noor also proposed a committee of specialists to assume responsibility for the conservation of architectural heritage and the proper review of designs for new public buildings and spaces.

What was the Queen addressing and attempting to establish? Sound foundations and subsequent structures—so they could remain strong and serviceable for decades.

What does your life need? A sound foundation—built upon a belief system—and a subsequent mission, so the mission can stand for decades.

BUILDING A SUSTAINABLE FUTURE

Whether a foundation is tangible—like in a building—or intangible—like in your life—a foundation is essential to building and sustaining a future. What belief system you build upon is up to you—but you have to have this foundation.

Talk to anyone who has worked with Pat Hickman for any length of time, and you will hear, probably sooner rather than later, that his personal relationship with Jesus Christ is what drives him—and inspires him. That's his belief system—that's what moves him forward, both personally and professionally. That's the foundation upon which everything else happens in his life. It defines who he is and what he is willing to stand for in his world. It's the source of how he determines what is the right thing to do—in every situation. It is the foundation for his non-negotiables—the product of his belief system and a mission.

During one of our meetings, Pat told me:

> Early on in my career, I was working as vice president of one of the commercial loan departments at a Texas bank. I was instructed to change the terms on a loan I had negotiated with a customer. I had quoted the customer a certain loan rate, and my boss told me to increase that loan rate in the small print.
>
> I remember he looked at me and said, "The customer will never notice. Go ahead and change the final documentation and have him sign it."
>
> I knew that wasn't in line with what I believed. All I could think of to say to him was, "What if he complains about it?"
>
> My boss said that was easy. He actually told me, "Should the customer complain, blame the girls in loan ops for typing in the wrong, higher rate—fix it to the agreed upon rate, and then change the rate back to the higher number when the customer leaves! In other words, don't just lie and deceive once, but twice!"
>
> I said, "I can't do that. I already told him what the rate would be. That's what I have to give him." We looked

each other over. And I left his office and handed everything over to the loan documentation people.

Later, when I went to pick the paperwork up, I saw that my boss had gone to loan documentation and told them to up the rate. I took a look at the paperwork, walked right back to the loan closure people, and said, "Change it back the to way my application said."

They said, "Yeah, but we were specifically instructed to do it this way."

I said, "You know what, I'll answer for that. You put it back the way I told you to do it, and if anybody says anything, just tell them I was the one who told you to put the numbers so they matched the application."

I know my boss looked at the final loan after I changed the terms back to where they were supposed to be. If he had challenged me on what I had done, my next move was going to be, "OK, I'm out. I quit." I guess he could tell I was willing to be fired over it, because he never said a word to me.

> **I believe that hidden deep within the deepest meaning of the word *belief* are the words *conviction, trust,* and *faith*. Transparency, authenticity, and integrity are constantly in my field of focus. Those are the attributes I continually work on living as non-negotiables.**

IF THE BELIEF SYSTEM IS SOUND, IT WILL INSPIRE OTHERS

We may decide, as Pat did, that it's worth getting fired to live what we believe, to do what our own belief system tells us to do.

Embedded deep within Pat's belief system is something that told him exactly what his next move was. It was something that said, "Do unto others as you would have them do unto you."

This idea is in the Torah, in the Quran, in the Tao Te Ching, and in the Hindu Mahabharata, too, but what you just read is how Jesus Christ stated it. Sages and teachers in all religious traditions have said more or less the same thing. For Pat, it matters that Jesus Christ said that, and it matters on a personal level that he follow that guidance. For you, it might be something or someone else.

Whatever you identify as the source of your belief system, you will know it really *is* your source when it inspires you to ask, and answer, the all-important question, "What's the right thing for me to do here?"

Some people use the word *belief* as though it's a moving target. I believe that hidden deep within the deepest meaning of the word *belief* are the words *conviction*, *trust*, and *faith*. That kind of belief means you don't sway when something or someone pulls at you. That kind of belief is absolute, and it is a rock solid foundation. When your beliefs are powerful and consistent enough to serve as the foundation of your life, that's when you have the greatest strength. Do your beliefs hold true under pressure? Are they still your beliefs when you find yourself face to face with the harshest events of your day? Or the toughest decisions to make?

WE DEFINE OUR BELIEFS, THEN OUR BELIEFS DEFINE US

When I speak about non-negotiables with organizations or community groups, there always seems to be one or more people who come up to me and ask, "What if I don't know what I believe?" or "What if my beliefs change?"

These are deep, searching questions. I can see in the eyes of the people who are sharing these thoughts with me that they want more clarity. They sincerely want substantive answers. I sense they feel a bit confused or unclear in their life, or that they may be lacking direction. Clarity provides acceleration to your journey. Lack of clarity is like putting the brakes on. You can't make progress on your goals and dreams when you're confused or in a fog.

> **Pat's belief system is the source of who he is and what he is willing to stand for in his world. It's his foundation.**

Many times we imagine that we don't know what we believe, but we really do know. Our actions reveal what we believe right now. What we have today is the result of decisions we made yesterday—decisions that reflect what we believe—whether we realize it or not.

And many times we know what we want to believe, but it's actually a situation where we are afraid to commit to our beliefs. Maybe we're afraid of what we'll have to give up. Maybe we're afraid we can't live up to some high standard and that we'll fail. Maybe we're afraid of what others might think of us or of the belief we choose to live. These are fears that we must face and overcome. I recommend you move forward even if you *feel* afraid. You only fail if you refuse to take a step.

Sometimes, there are people who just don't know what they believe and they are still struggling. If that describes you, you should know that there comes a point in life where you have to make some choices. You make choices, and then you commit and move forward. That is what believing is all about. It's a commitment.

Are you willing to commit? Are you willing to say that you stand for something and then do what you say? You can say that you're a team player, that you believe in people, that you want to do what you know is right and so on, but if your actions betray you, then everyone will know whether or not that is what you really believe.

When you believe something you trust it, you rely on it, you credit it, and you follow it. You may not always make the right decisions or the best decisions around what you believe, but when you really believe something, then you move quickly to correct any mistakes that you make. You always do what is right around what you believe.

We are all human. We all make mistakes, but when we really believe something, then we acknowledge what happened, correct it, and move on.

YOU CAN ALWAYS MAKE A COURSE CORRECTION

Making adjustments in life along the journey is a constant in a healthy life—and it applies to everything we've talked about thus far in this book, especially your beliefs. For instance, just like whatever is non-negotiable in your life, your beliefs must respect the rights of others. History has provided proof over and over again that when we build belief systems on hate, fear, or lack of respect, that belief system won't work. A belief system that doesn't value people is a severely faulted belief system—one that will lead to failure on many levels.

> **Organizations that focus on tactics do well. Organizations that focus on people do phenomenally well.**

Sometimes people are afraid to specify what they believe because they think doing so means sacrificing something they've grown accustomed to in life. This is a myth. When we commit to a belief system, we really aren't giving up anything. The truth is that we are gaining control, and that is huge. We're setting a course.

We all know perspective can change over time. In our younger years we may get a job just so we can afford to rent a little apartment, buy a used car, pay for gas and insurance, and maybe a little entertainment. After our formal education is complete, we may be working to pay off debt, buy our first home, or support a new family. Later in life, we may change our perspective and look to our professional life as a way to not only earn a living, but also as a way to make a difference in a specific area of personal concern.

It's good to go through these periods of growth. It's good to question and seek answers. Just going through this process brings affirmation, clarity, and certainty, which can be very comforting. A great belief system can serve you through all of these changes and stages of life. A great belief system doesn't change just because situations change.

Your beliefs may be rooted in the teachings of your parents, in something you read that moved you deeply, or in your spiritual life. Everyone is different. Your belief system may be based on religious scripture, as Pat's is, or on another source of your choosing. You could simply live your life by what you learned in kindergarten and how to get along in the sandbox. Whatever beliefs you build on, you need to make sure they work, and you need to be all-in committed. You need to know that it's OK to have the freedom to stand on what you believe, both individually and as a company. You need to have beliefs so that you know whether you are hitting the mark or not.

Taking the time to stop and think about what you believe is key to leading a successful life and career. Determining ahead of time—before life or organizations throw you a curveball—what you believe directly affects the outcome of any situation. It affects whether you go through an experience in control or out of control.

Collectively, as individuals and organizations, if we don't know where we're going—because we don't know what we believe—we can end up anywhere rather than where we want to land. Knowing what you believe empowers you to land somewhere intentionally. We have to be intentional in our decision making. We have to be aware of our choices—and the trajectory of their consequences.

In South Texas there is a river that has overflown its banks many times with the swell of spring rains. The Guadalupe is a favorite of kayakers, canoeing and tubing enthusiasts, and white water rafters. It typically becomes much too dangerous and often takes lives each time it floods—with the release of water from Canyon Dam. Authorities close it to such recreational activities to protect lives once it races at 1200 cfs (cubic feet per second). You may have seen national news stories through the years showing the familiar sight of helicopters rescuing stranded tourists from treetops.

But when the Guadalupe is manageable for recreation, it has the power to take people where it wants to go—unless they maneuver against the current. For years the current has carved a path over boulders, around bends, and against banks of exposed black earth and mangled tree roots. If you enter the river and exert no effort against the current, you will go wherever its path leads—nowhere intentional on your behalf. You will be driven by its power, and the trajectory of your landing will be out of your control.

On the other hand, if you intentionally swim, canoe, or kayak where you want to go, your destination will be determined by you—but it requires conscious effort. It takes studying the river and its course. It takes a predetermination of will, thought, and decision making to carve out your own path and subsequent destinations all along the river's route.

Once we start acting in accordance with our beliefs, not just talking about them, we start operating on a higher plane, and those standards can actually become part of who we are.

Taking the time to define what you believe about personal matters (life, death, marriage, family, spirituality, success, right vs. wrong) and professional matters (your career, your work ethic, your company, how you treat people, your relationship with coworkers and customers) determines the trajectory of your life. If you want to land somewhere satisfying, fulfilling, purposeful, intentional, then you will have to define your beliefs and subsequent mission. You can't leave it to the river of life and how fast it's flowing. You can't leave it to natural forces and unpredictable bends and eroding boulders. You have to get your heart and head involved in defining your belief system.

All belief has a beginning—a genesis of evolution—whether it's yours personally or your company's. Yours is defined by events, emotional evidence, your upbringing, education, culture, and other influences. It begins with all the things you were taught as a child, that you evaluated and questioned as a young adult, that you ultimately determined as your own. If not, this is the process I'm challenging you to define now. In fact, even if you think you have a great foundational belief system, evaluate it. This might be a good juncture in life to reaffirm or make a course adjustment.

In the same way, your company's beliefs have been defined by its leaders and their values—or you if you are the leader of the company. And it's not about what you say, but what you do and what you lead your teams to do—whether consciously or not.

I remember being in eighth grade in a mechanical drawing class, and the teacher posed a question like this: Do businesses exist to make money or provide value?

I was 13, so of course I responded by saying businesses existed to make money! Here's my point: I've always remembered that grade school experience because it started an awareness in me that I didn't buy into until decades later—businesses exist to provide value and service.

Money is not a purpose. Businesses exist to provide value, and if they do it well, they are able to generate money...to stay in business. It's a cycle, but it begins with deciding what you believe. If you believe you're in business to make money, you will ultimately fail. If you believe you're in business to provide a valuable product or service, you will make money.

Personally, I've made decisions to make money—and they are the places where I lost the most money. Later, I made decisions to create value—and that's where I made the most money. I didn't know what I believed, so I had no control and no success. Once I did define what I believed and purposed to produce value, growth occurred. What you believe matters and sets the course for your life. And whether you feel like you have control over anything or not, you do have control over what you believe.

A SHARED BELIEF SYSTEM PRODUCES COLLECTIVE ACTIONS

It's time to slow down and think about what you believe— and why you believe it. Look at your life. Reflect. Is it rooted in what you learned from someone who inspired you by his or her personal example? Is it rooted in your past experiences and subsequent evaluations and decisions?

What is your foundation? Your foundation is what inspires your decisions—and is evidenced by your actions.

It's the same with an organization. Out of what kind of foundation was it birthed? What beliefs does it reflect? Is it focused on value that produces money? Or money that compromises value?

A culture is nothing more or less than a shared belief system that expresses itself in action.

Whatever your day-to-day actions and decision-making techniques are, they reflect your beliefs. In other words, you have some whether you realize it or not—and so does your company.

71

You have to get in touch with what you believe consciously. Consciously is an important state of mind. It leads to intentionality, which is purposeful. You need to know what you believe purposefully.

This is evident at Happy State Bank. They don't sit around and try to think of what they believe with every challenge or question that arises. They don't struggle—ever. Their beliefs mimic those of Pat Hickman—and every employee knows the non-negotiables that come from those beliefs. It's all settled and the course is set.

Happy State Bank's non-negotiables are grounded in truth. Everyone's need to be. Truth is that substance and foundation we build our lives on that doesn't change. Situations may change, but truth doesn't. If it was truth yesterday, it's truth today and tomorrow. Truth doesn't fail. We may. After all, we are human. But truth is like gravity—it doesn't change, regardless of our opinions. Absolutes—non-negotiables—don't change, and they empower you to weather storms and make it through.

Happy State Bank illustrates this so well. As you'll truly see in the stories I share later in this book, the bank has done a great job of recognizing you must treat people in a certain way, you must truly value them—employees and customers alike—to succeed, and that's an absolute, a truth that will never change. It's a truth that stems from how Pat Hickman, as the CEO, lives his life personally and professionally—and that is a critical component to his successful life of living non-negotiables. It's easy for staff members to follow Pat Hickman. His behavior and expectations are very clear. He doesn't do one thing and live another. Nothing is fuzzy.

Usually, when we find ourselves inspired by a person, for example, and we look closely at *why* we are inspired, we find that it has something to do with what the person has identified as non-negotiable in his or her life. Maybe it was their quality of life, the way they treated others, or the level of excellence they required of themselves and others.

When people take action in support of what they truly believe, deep down inside, that attracts our attention. Think of leaders like Martin Luther King, Jr. or Mahatma Gandhi, or the founding fathers of the United States. All of these people were willing to be put in jail, and even willing to face death, in order to act in full accordance with what they believed.

> **Every life—and every company—needs standards. They spur us on to greatness and inspire better lives and companies. They produce decisions that lead to positive control.**

A lot of times, though, we look at our own lives and find that our actions just plain don't meet the high standards of the people we admire most. We don't back up our own words about what we say we believe. We don't want to be accountable to people. That doesn't make us bad. It just makes us unaccountable. As a result, what we "believe" changes, based on the situation.

An amazing thing happens, though, once we begin asking, "What's the right thing for me to do?" Once we identify our beliefs and then start *acting* in accordance with our beliefs, not just talking about them, we start operating on a higher plane, and those standards can actually become part of who we are. They can also inspire others to be more accountable to other people, and they can even lead an organization to embrace a culture that inspires accountability. I know that Pat has greatly inspired me on this front, because he has built an organization that challenges everyone who encounters it to fully align their beliefs with their actions.

Drayton McLane, Jr. is a former vice-chairman of Walmart and a former owner of the Houston Astros. He is also a member of Pat's board of directors. In discussing Happy State Bank's commitment to accountability, Drayton McLane told me:

"Accountability is the most difficult word in the English language. We don't know how to spell it, we don't know how to identify what it is, and we don't like any part of it. We like it in others, but we don't like it in ourselves."

What Pat models is a belief system that he is willing to be personally accountable for, all the time, and that's what makes all the difference.

Once people really understand what your belief system is, and once there's respect in play based on the actions they have seen you take to live those beliefs, then people are far more likely to raise their game to your actions. Sometimes they will do this even though they have very different belief systems from yours! They will aim to model your level of integrity, even if they don't want to model your specific beliefs. This is not proselytizing. It is making everyone around you better.

Drayton McLane also told me: "Pat's formal job title is that of CEO. That means he is there to set the mission, to set the tone for the overall level of service, to inspire people to execute his vision, and so on. But his real job is to preserve the culture. Most people don't understand that."

A culture is a shared belief system that expresses itself in action.

Once your actions match up with a sound belief system and it is clear *from your actions* that you are upholding that belief system, you can expect some of the people you interact with to respect you and even look up to you more than they did before. But that's not the main reason to identify and live by a sound belief system. The main reason to identify and live by a sound belief system is that *life works better when you do that.*

If you raise your own game, you really can inspire others to want to raise theirs. I realize that may sound simple and familiar, and I realize that a lot of people act as though what I've just shared is simple "common sense," but very few of us seem to have sense enough to make it common practice in our lives and our organizations! In part, that's because so few of us have ever had a good role model who showed us what it looked like when somebody both talks the talk *and* walks the walk. Our role model might say to be honest, but when they aren't charged for an item at the checkout, they don't bring it to the cashier's attention.

> **Once your actions match up with a sound belief system and it is clear from your actions that you are upholding a higher standard, you can expect some of the people you interact with to respect you and even look up to you more than they did before. But that's not the main reason to identify and live by a sound belief system. The main reason to identify and live by a sound belief system is that life works better when you do that.**

Pat Hickman isn't that kind of person. He talks the talk *and* walks the walk, and that's why I'm conducting an in-depth examination of his personal example. Notice that I'm not suggesting that you have to reach the same conclusions as Pat has about what your belief system should be—only that you notice the powerful impact this man's life has had on others because he knows when and where he draws the line. He knows what he believes. If you choose to adopt the exact same belief system that he does, that's fine. If you don't, he's still going to be clear with you and the rest of the world about exactly where he stands. And his example will inspire you to build one that will work for you.

Consider this example of how Pat lives his belief system—and subsequent mission and non-negotiables:

A while back, Happy State Bank bought a bank in another city, and Pat and his team went down there for a board meeting. Pat makes a point of beginning his meetings with a prayer of thanks to God Almighty and Jesus Christ. He has never apologized for doing that. It's just part of who he is.

After the meeting, Pat got word that one of the members of the board—a non-Christian woman—had taken exception to the prayer, and specifically to Pat's mention of Jesus.

When Pat heard about her reaction, he made a conscious decision not to just let the incident go by the wayside. He decided that he wanted to talk to this woman, face to face.

So after the board meeting, he called her and scheduled a time to meet with her at her home. When he arrived, she welcomed him, and they had a very a nice, very civil conversation. Pat told her that he wanted to hear her concerns on what had happened at the beginning of the meeting.

She told him how she felt about that prayer he'd said. Pat heard her out and thanked her for sharing her feelings. Then he told her his side.

"I certainly didn't want to offend you or anyone else," he said. "I do want you to know that when I got started in my career, I made a personal commitment to give thanks to Jesus Christ for everything God allowed me to accomplish. And I made a personal commitment to acknowledge God in absolutely everything I do. Now as far as the meetings go, if you decide that it's appropriate for you to show up a few minutes late, after the prayer is over, I would understand that and I would have absolutely no problem with that. But I have an obligation to acknowledge God in everything I do. It would *kill* me not to do that."

Offering a prayer of thanks is part of Pat's belief system. It's just who he is. Notice that he *was not* trying to get this woman to accept his spiritual practice as her own. He was explaining *who he was as a person*. That's the nature of a belief system. It defines you—not just some of the time, but all of the time.

After Pat was done, the board member smiled and said she understood and even said that she respected Pat for his convictions. The two parted happily. There was no longer any problem to solve.

Am I saying you have to adopt Pat's belief system? Of course not! What I am saying, though, is that if something is not based on your personal belief system, not based in who you *are*, it can't possibly be developed into a non-negotiable.

I believe you'll agree when you see how Happy State Bank's 20 non-negotiables, that follow in Part Two of this book, are applied to how the bank is run on a daily basis. You'll see how each one lines up with Pat's personal relationship with Jesus Christ and his commitment to, "Do unto others as you would have them do unto you."

If you walk your talk—if you identify and stand behind a compelling *mission* and a compelling list of personal non-negotiables that are totally aligned with your personal belief system—it doesn't matter whether others share your specific beliefs! It matters that you live by them. A life of accountability and a company culture that inspires accountability will be the natural outflow. Remember, the Power of Accountability™ is when you know what you believe, what your mission is, what is in your control, and what is truly non-negotiable for you—and everyone on your team understands and lives by those non-negotiables—you will create an environment where people can be their very best both for themselves and the organization. The natural outflow is a place where accountability is abundant and people keep their commitments to themselves and to others.

You may not be the head of your company or division or department. But you are the head of your life. Implement these truths in the areas of life where you can, and watch positive change and momentum begin.

Pat Hickman opened the door of possibility and purpose for his whole organization, and for me, with the sheer power of his personal example. His commitment to his belief system caused me to look deeper into my own belief system, so that I make choices based on that system and my commitment to it. Here's a guy who lives his life by what he believes. He carries with him, everywhere he goes, an important lesson: When you really believe something, you do it.

> It is truly freeing to be at a point in life when you know what you really believe. There are many things I no longer have to question. My proactive decision making of building a foundation comprised of standards, beliefs, mission, and non-negotiables has given me control, and that control has yielded freedom.

My actions tell you exactly what I believe, not what I want to believe. I have to consciously work daily to ensure that those actions and beliefs are in alignment. Transparency, authenticity, and integrity are constantly in my field of focus. Those are the attributes I continually work on living as non-negotiables. They're my target. Now, the nice thing about having a target is this: Either you hit a target or you don't. If you don't, you acknowledge that and you aim again.

I have discovered an amazing freedom at this point in my personal journey: It is truly freeing to be at a point in life where you know what you really believe. There are many things I no longer have to question. If you think about efficiency, it's living an efficient life. By knowing what I believe, I make decisions more easily and I move forward. I'm not stuck. I'm not bogged down in any mire. I know what I believe, and I do it—every day.

5

VALUING PEOPLE

At the very heart of who Pat is, is a person who truly values people. Pat recognizes that one of the major reasons he has achieved success is that he has surrounded himself with amazing people. The interesting part is that Pat sees amazing traits in everyone. He recognizes their potential. He places people in positions that may be entirely new to them, but Pat believes that they will thrive in those positions. I have spoken with many people at Happy State Bank who have been more than emotional as they expressed their thanks for what they have become both professionally and personally because Pat believed in them and put them in a place where their potential could flourish.

Additionally, I noticed how Pat was just as comfortable talking with a janitor as he was a vice-president of the bank. It struck me that Pat truly values people. Pat believes that everyone has worth, that everyone has strengths and weaknesses, and that everyone has the ability to contribute to the bank, their family, and the community.

When people are valued they feel it. They know and feel that they are valued. People who feel valued do not want to let others down. They do not want to do anything that would diminish that value. There is an exchange that takes place between people and a change inside an organization where everyone wants to be better.

I asked Pat about whether he had people who might have been somewhat aimless but came under his wing and he had opened up opportunities for. He responded with: "I've actually had several spouses come up to me over the years and say, 'Thank you, my spouse, husband, wife, is a better person since they worked at Happy State Bank. My husband is smiling more than I've ever seen him smile before. My wife is smiling more. Our kids like their daddy better because he works at Happy State Bank.' I bet I've had that said to me 150 to 200 times. I don't know. I've had people go to me and say, 'Don't you worry about my son ever leaving your bank because I'd kill him first.'"

Recently we did a project for a large company. When we start a relationship with a new client we usually do an "uptake" survey to clearly identify the current strengths and weaknesses of the organization from an accountability, leadership, and culture aspect. We discovered right away that while the organization was making money, the people working there would not recommend working at this company to their family and friends. This is a powerful statement to how they don't feel valued in this organization. This lack of feeling valued leads to a lack of engagement, absence of accountability, greater turnover, lower productivity, and reduced profits.

NO WORDS NECESSARY

> **When people are valued they feel it. There is an exchange that takes place between people and a change inside an organization where everyone wants to be better.**

We may think that we value people because we tell them we value them, we tell them that we appreciate what they do, or we tell them that they are important. And, while taking the time to share those thoughts is important, words alone don't convey the real intent of valuing people. Just because you tell someone you value them does not make it so. Just because you speak it does not make it truth. It's not what you say that really shows someone that you value them, it's what you do. Actions speak volumes.

Every year right before Christmas, Happy State Bank gives out their bonuses. In some organizations the bonus check is included in with your regular check. In some organizations the department manager hands out the bonus check. At Happy State Bank Pat goes to every one of his branches and hands the bonus check to everyone personally. Pat takes the time to show each person that he cares, that he appreciates what he or she does for the bank and that he values each and every one of them. When the president of a company shows up to hand you your bonus check, you feel different. You feel valued. At Happy State Bank it's not about the bonus check. Pat could have shown up and said that there wasn't going to be a bonus check this year and everyone would have still felt valued. It's all about the fact that Pat took the time to come see each person. When you take time out of your life to show that their life is important to you, you are valuing people.

When you value something, you show that it is important. If you value your car, you might wash it and keep it clean. If you value a painting, you might hang it in a prominent place in your home and even shine a spotlight on the painting so everyone can see it in its best light. You value your family and you make sure they are fed and you personally sacrifice so they don't have to. You never have to say anything if your actions are in alignment with what you say you believe. Your actions tell the entire story.

EVERYONE HAS VALUE

How many times have we seen someone who is very eager to speak with a "bigwig" in an organization but doesn't have the time of day for someone who "appears" unimportant? There are some who are only willing to engage in conversation when they think they will gain some benefit from it. This type of behavior is a direct reflection of someone who does not truly value people. They only value the people whom they think can help them get something or go somewhere.

It is up to us to find the potential in all people and then help them unleash that potential. It should never be about us. It is always about the other person. When you value people, you not only recognize their potential but you work to help them fulfill that potential. You are looking at how you can serve them, not how they can serve you. You are "other people" centric rather than "me" centric.

When you value people, everyone has value and you gain great joy in helping them feel valued and reaching their potential. Leaders know how to look at someone and say, "I know that this is what you can be." Leaders see something in everyone and then go about putting them in a position and allowing them to go do it.

PEOPLE TRY TO CONTROL PEOPLE

We see in many organizations where some people try to control the people around them rather than valuing those individuals. They try to control them with money, the promise of promotion, fear, and the use of their position on the organizational chart. When you are trying to control people, you strip them of their sense of worth, and when you do that they do not feel valued.

I frequently hear, "I pay them more so I expect them to do more." That is an example of trying to control people with money rather than trying to motivate people to be their best because they feel important to the mission of the organization. Most leaders who say this do not even realize that they are trying to control people with money. They do not understand where their thinking is wrong.

There is a difference between rewarding someone for a job well done and holding something over a person's head in an attempt to control them and get certain results. I'm amazed at the so-called leaders who employ this tactic all the time.

WE ARE ALL THE SAME

All people have the same needs. We have the same fears and concerns. We need to eat. We need shelter. We need to be safe. We want to provide for our families. We want to love and be loved. We need to feel a sense of worth.

We may come from different backgrounds, geographic areas, or religious beliefs. We may act different, look different, or even sound different. But we are all human beings. We all have value. No one is greater or less than anyone else. Our parent's name doesn't make us better or the amount of money in our bank account or the car we drive. Our home address doesn't make us less than anyone else and neither does our job or the amount of education that we may or may not have. Many times when someone asks another person, "What do you do for a living?" they are just starting the process of judging that individual and determining whether to raise or lower the amount of value they think that person has. We tend to want to put people in a nice little package based on those things. Rather than starting a conversation off by asking someone, "What do you do?" or "Where do you live?" why not try, "So tell me about Bill." Put the person in a position to share what is really important to them. Show them you value who they are and what they want to share.

When we start judging people by any of these issues, we are not valuing people. When we say, "All people from that place are lazy," then we are generalizing, making judgments, and not valuing people equally.

I was at dinner with a group of people. The guy across the table started talking about a particular individual. He said, "I can't believe that guy had that level of clearance with a government agency; he's a junior college dropout." As soon as the words left his mouth I knew it was wrong. He made a generalizing statement and that always devalues people. Sharon was sitting to my right and one of us was going to say something. Sharon spoke up first and said, "He's obviously a very smart guy. I know a lot of people who have graduated from four-year universities and they're not very smart." The guy across the table from us was saying something that was devaluing of an individual, particularly when he didn't know anything about the individual. It was wrong.

I once had a client say before a speech, "Just keep it simple. This group hasn't graduated college. One or two good ideas is great." This leader didn't realize that he was devaluing people. He was placing limitations on their ability and on his thinking. As a leader you are going to lead people based on what you believe about them. If you believe they have great potential, you will lead them to achieve their potential. They will benefit, your organization will benefit, and the people you are leading will respect you even more.

How many times do we say something about a person and it's a generalization and we don't even know if it's true or not? When someone devalues an individual it's usually because they are trying to elevate themselves. Putting someone down doesn't make us better. You cannot be an effective, accountable leader and create an accountable culture if you devalue people.

It is easy to fall into this trap, but it is a trap we must avoid. The person living on the street has just as much value as the CEO of some big company. We just may not know what that value is unless we take the time to find out. And, while you walk down the street and pass judgment on that homeless person, stop and remember that you know nothing about them. You don't know their life's story, you don't know if they are a high school dropout or a college graduate, you have no idea as to what they may have accomplished and why they may have ended up or chosen, that's right chosen, to live on the street.

> **Leaders see something in everyone and then go about putting them in a position and allowing them to go do it.**

THE RICHNESS OF VALUING PEOPLE

When you see a difference in people, you are discriminating. When you see a difference, you are allowing that difference to impact what you think about that person and that is not valuing people. That is deciding who has value and who doesn't. I realize this is a tough area and that many of us may not have the best habits here, but we must make an effort to change. Diversity doesn't just happen in our world. We have to do it on purpose. It's easy to hang out with people because they look like you; go to the same church, mosque, or synagogue as you; or have the same beliefs as you. Diversity can make your life richer. Diversity opens up your view of people and the world. It helps you really understand what it means to value people.

The power of valuing people comes down to looking for ways to encourage them. Valuing people translates into encouraging everyone around you. Encouraging people changes lives and unlocks potential. This is not about getting anything for you. It is all about what you can give others. When you are talking about accountability, you have to leave your stereotypes, biases, and prejudices at the door. There can be no accountability without valuing people.

There is a significant difference in working in an environment where people are controlled versus where people are valued. As we move forward through the other three elements of building a culture that promotes, supports, and inspires accountability, it is critical to know that everything rests on this foundation of valuing people.

6

DISCOVERING WHAT'S IN YOUR CONTROL

Early on in our study of Happy State Bank we noticed that they were different. I'm sure you already gathered that. The attitude of the workers was different. The amount of perceived stress in the workplace was different, and definitely lower than any other high performance organization we had worked with. And the focus of the people was different. It was apparent that not only were all of the employees very focused but their focus led to results.

Like any organization, challenges arise at Happy, and like any organization, people have to deal with those challenges. What became apparent very quickly was that the employees at Happy always focus on those areas that they have control over. This caused me to think about other clients and organizations I was familiar with. How many times over the years have I heard, "The economy is bad. It's different in our region. Our competitors have great products. Politicians just don't get it. The 'other' party is in office." It goes on and on. All of those statements may or may not be true, but the one fact that is true is that none of those issues are in your control. Spending time thinking about, worrying about, or focusing on issues that just aren't in our control is simply a waste of time. That time spent will not move you closer to solving your challenges and reaching your goals.

I also noticed that when people make excuses in our world they almost always make them around instances they can't control rather than focusing on what they can control and getting positive results. "I'm sorry I'm late, there was traffic on the way to work." You can't control the traffic but you can control what time you leave. "I'm behind on getting your house finished because of my laborers, the weather, the inspectors, the grasshoppers." Enough already! *No More Excuses!*

When you eliminate focusing on things you can't control, you will eliminate the excuses in your life. When you eliminate excuses you start to look for solutions. When you look for solutions, you look at what you can control and make decisions in those areas. When you make decisions in the areas you can control you get results.

FOUR AREAS OF CONTROL TO THINK ABOUT

What is in your control is your way of thinking. It really does come down to how you think. You have to believe you can control something before you can. You have to be able to recognize what is actually in your control.

Things You Can Control

The first thing you can control are your beliefs. In the last chapter we talked about those. Next look at your life or at your business and think about what is in your control. There are the tactical elements we can control and there are non-tactical. Some tactical procedures you can control are:

- How you hire employees
- How you train employees
- Designing the products and services you offer
- The company branding

The list is endless.

Where I find that many organizations and people come up short is in the non-tactical areas they can control. Some of those are:

- Choosing a leadership style that revolves around serving others
- What you think about
- Your beliefs
- How you treat people

Whether tactical or non-tactical, the things you can control are significant to your success. In any given situation where you need to solve a problem, start off stating the challenge and then asking, "What is in my control?" When you list everything you can control, you will find you know the answers to your problem.

I also noticed that when people make excuses in our world, they almost always make them around things they can't control.

Things You Can't Control

There are many elements we cannot control. Some of them are:

- Economy
- Competition
- Government
- Technology
- The world around us

When we focus on these issues, we will always come up short, because it is impossible to solve any problem in an area we can't control. But for every item we can't control, there are a host of related areas we can. We may not be able to control the economy, but we can control how we advertise in a down market. We can control the way we develop our staff. We can control the creativity used to put together the services we offer. We can provide unique financing for our clients. The list of what we can control may seem endless as it relates to a single area we can't, so it is amazing why so many people choose to focus on the wrong issues.

> **What is in your control is your way of thinking. It really does come down to how you think. You have to believe you can control something before you can.**

People who focus on what they cannot control make excuses. People who focus on what they can control get results. People who focus on what they cannot control get bogged down. People who focus on what they can control move forward.

Things You Try to Control

It's not uncommon for someone to be stuck because they are attempting the impossible feat of trying to control something that they simply can't control. The most common example of this is people. When you try to control people, you very rarely achieve the result you are looking for. When you tell someone they have to be accountable, do you consistently receive the behavior you are looking for? Really, what you can control is the culture you create within an organization that *encourages* someone to want to be accountable.

Sometimes we try to control people with money. We feel that because we are paying them we control what they do or we control their loyalty when, in fact, if someone paid them more money, that person would leave. If you are doing the right things and treating people the right way, they will want to be there and they won't leave even if offered more money. It is in this environment that your business will thrive. We all need money, but for most people money is not their sole motivator. People will stay some place where they love what they do and love who they do it with. Rather than trying to control people with money, work to let people know they are appreciated, important, and an integral part of your future. I once heard someone say they wanted to work someplace they feel celebrated. That is the environment you should be working to achieve.

Things That Are Out of Control

It is not uncommon to have some area in our organization or our life that is out of control. Examples are:

- Expenses
- Payroll
- Relationships
- Activities your children are engaged in

Only when we look for and recognize that something is out of control can we take action to get it back in control.

> **People who focus on what they cannot control make excuses. People who focus on what they can control get results. People who focus on what they cannot control get bogged down. People who focus on what they can control move forward.**

There may be some areas out of control that we might not normally think of. Leadership could be out of control. Think about the situation at Enron where the executives were hiding their losses and employees and investors lost entire retirement portfolios. Or look at Tyko where the CEO was using corporate funds to buy expensive art. Or think about some of the investment institutions and banks and their ill-advised choices.

Out-of-control leadership allowed those organizations to create a lot of harm for the people they were supposed to be serving, both internally and externally.

Leadership can get out of control by letting some people come in late while they don't let other people get away with it. That is not an employee getting out of control. That is inconsistent leadership. When you have great leadership it is evident. Great leaders don't try to control their people. Inconsistent leadership doesn't happen at Happy State Bank, and it will not happen at any organization where people really want to be a part of the culture.

THE CONNECTION TO NON-NEGOTIABLES

You can't have a non-negotiable for something you can't control. It is critical to understand that we all have an immense amount of control in our life if we only take the time to understand where that control lies. It really does come down to focus and responsibility.

We must learn to focus on what we can control and not let the popular issues in our world that we cannot control distract us, our lives, and our organizations. We must also learn to take the responsibility to make decisions with those areas we actually can control. That means not abdicating and giving up control. When we give up control we are usually denying our own personal responsibility and we are relegating our success to the whims of someone else.

When you combine a knowledge of what you believe with what you can control, you are positioned to create a non-negotiable in your life or business that will allow you to achieve your mission.

7

Finding Your Mission—
Your Public Declaration
of Purpose

When the United States was attacked by terrorists and planes were intentionally flown into the Twin Towers in New York City on 9/11, former President George W. Bush addressed the nation later in the day from the Oval Office. He said, "A great people has been moved to defend a great nation. Terrorist attacks can shake the foundations of our biggest buildings, but they cannot touch the foundation of America. These acts shatter steel, but they cannot dent the steel of American resolve."

The foundation of two buildings was tangible, but the foundation of America—its resolve as President Bush defined it—was intangible, yet unshakeable despite such a historic and horrific attack. We saw in the following weeks after the attacks that as a nation of many peoples, we may have been politically polarized, but the majority of us shared our nation's collective values. We agreed on protecting our nation—our friends, families, and neighbors. We were united in our mission—our public declaration of purpose—to maintain who we are and what we hold dear, and to fight and defend what others have paid a high price for—our freedom.

Mission brings clarity for individuals and groups, like a nation or corporation. It brings unity of focus. It is your declaration of purpose—or the purpose of your company. Even if intangible, it is no less powerful than a foundation that holds tons and tons of steel framing. It's an invisible force, birthed out of a personal belief system, that motivates and drives people beyond what they ever imagined possible. It can often be put into words, as you'll see with Happy State Bank, but it isn't always tangible. How it's lived out is what becomes tangible. Its existence is evidenced in its results. In Chapter 1, I said Pat Hickman filled the room with his presence, with his sense of a serious personal goal. What I saw was a man with purpose and a mission—on a mission.

> **There's something magical when a company will actually believe its mission statement and just do it! It's not enough to just write a great one—you have to live it. The application of a mission statement makes the difference.**

One of the very first missions I had in life started as only a dream in high school. I'm a runner and I first started running as a teenager. Back then, a competitive race was 2.2 miles. Today, a 5K is typical for a high school level. At that point in my life, running a marathon was unthinkable for me. Running something as competitive as the Boston Marathon—the only marathon outside the Olympic trials that you have to qualify for—was beyond comprehension—but it was a dream.

Through the years, I continued to enjoy recreational running—a few miles every few days—until the day I was sitting at my son's first little league game. (He's now 31.) A man in front me was wearing a T-shirt that read he was in training for the New York City Marathon. We had just moved to this new neighborhood, and after meeting him I learned he lived a few doors down. He had heard I was a runner and invited me to train and run with him, but I didn't think I could be in training for anything! My knees had bothered me and I figured anything more challenging was out of the question.

But the morning after I met my new neighbor, I awoke at the crack of dawn with our conversation running through my mind. I couldn't get the idea of a marathon out of my head. I went out the front door and ran six miles.

I later called him and said, "I'm in!"

Soon, I began training with him. We researched and read, and put together a schedule that was rigorous—and we stuck to it, rain or shine. We were committed. We ran every time we could, everywhere we could. We ran on indoor tracks, outside trails, treadmills at the gym—literally every time we could run, no matter the weather.

We ran some 10K races...and my time began to look better and better. We began to project what our time would be to run in a marathon. So we grew even more serious. A mission began to develop—a sense of a serious personal goal—to run the Boston Marathon. What once had been only a teenage dream was taking shape and becoming a true mission.

We began training at a pace that would support a four-hour race—and our times kept dropping. I entered the New York City Marathon with my friend and made every mistake possible! I crashed and burned the last six miles, but I learned a lot—including the reality that I could actually run such a race! My time was 3:20. I needed 3:15 to qualify for my age group for Boston! We had blown through the four-hour time goal.

I ran the Grandma's Marathon in Duluth, Minnesota next—and I qualified for the Boston Marathon! If you're a runner, you can imagine how I felt.

From that point on, my mission was clear. Every decision I made was in support of getting to and accomplishing the Boston Marathon. Whether I was in town or in another country, I ran. I trained. I remember running in numerous cities where I didn't have any idea where I was going, but I never got lost and I always made it back to the hotel. Whether I was in Chicago or London, running had moved from being recreational in my life to a driving force. I was driven by an intangible mission that ensured tangible results.

I eventually qualified six years in a row for the Boston Marathon—including the 100th anniversary race. My mission took me far. My declared purpose determined my daily decisions and actions—and it produced.

MISSION DETERMINES RESULTS

The mission of Happy State bank reads: *Work hard, have fun, make money, while providing outstanding customer service and honoring the Golden Rule.*

This mission ties directly in to one of Pat's core beliefs. It's a core belief that serves as the foundation for everything he and his bank do, one that's impossible to forget, one that is very easy for just about anyone else to buy into, that at first is an intangible motivation: Do what's right. That's what the Golden Rule boils down to, after all: Do what's right.

> **Just like you are a parent to your kids, always teaching, guiding them in the way they should go—basically passing on your values on a very personal level and applying them to life—so an organization has to mentor its employees with its beliefs and mission—continually.**

As you will see, this principle drives everything Pat does—and leads to all the tangible acts he and his staff perform daily to carry out the mission. He is so committed to it that he and the executive team built it right in to the bank's mission, which is (as you know by now) the concise sentence that identifies his whole purpose, his reason for getting up in the morning. It sets out the bank's reason for existing. It's their public declaration of purpose. Pat's is publicly welded to the Golden Rule, to the idea of doing what's right by other people. That's one of the things that drew me to him when I first saw him in Amarillo.

Once one person takes on a commitment like that in a prominent, easy-to-remember way, and then honors that commitment, a kind of personal power emerges. This power is rooted in two things—a willingness to serve others and a great mission that you are ready, willing, and eager to talk about every day. Pat has both.

There is something magical about a mission birthed out of a clear belief system. There's something magical when a company will actually believe its mission statement and just do it! It's not enough to just write a great one—you have to live it. The application of a mission statement makes the difference.

At Happy State Bank, I saw that magic in action firsthand. In fact, that magic was what brought this book into existence. I signed on for this project when I realized that Pat's commitment to his mission not only drove him and shaped everything he did, but also drove his whole organization—and all their actions. The executive team spent a lot of time working on this one sentence, and it shows.

Because his mission backs up both who Pat is as a person and what his organization is all about, this sentence actually means something to the people who work at the bank. It is not just something that gets read aloud once at an annual meeting, or tacked up on a wall no one passes very often, or written in a memo and then forgotten. These words are the compass point of the man and the organization. They define who Pat is and what the bank is. They are a constant topic of conversation, a constant point of reference, a constant barometer for "how we do things around here."

I interviewed more than 100 Happy employees and met 200 more. One was a teller in the Borger, Texas branch. I asked her if she knew the mission statement. She did. This branch is approximately 50 miles from corporate, and she knew the mission. She wasn't a vice-president or even a branch manager. She wasn't in a management position where perhaps she was required to repeat the mission frequently. No, she was a demonstration of how committed the bank is to knowing and living its mission—on a daily basis.

Communication is the key. Just like you are a parent to your kids, always teaching, guiding them in the way they should go—basically passing on your values on a very personal level and applying them to life—so an organization has to mentor its employees with its beliefs and mission—continually.

YOU NEED ALL FIVE

I once asked Pat to describe his "onboarding" process to me—what he does to make sure the people he hires buy in to the bank's special culture and support it. At first, he said that I should talk to someone in his Human Resources department about their Happy Beginnings program, so I could get all the details of what someone's first week looked like—all the orientation sessions, all the training topics, and so forth.

"What I'm really interested in," I said, "is *your* personal interaction with the new hires. Do you make a point of connecting face to face with every new hire during that person's first week?"

"Well, sure," he said. "At the end of, or sometimes a few weeks after the Happy Beginnings program, we get everybody together and I spend some time with them talking about the mission statement. That's important."

So here's the way it works: If you get hired by this bank—if they think you're a "Happy person"—the very first thing of consequence that happens once you finish your on-board program is you get face time with the founder of the bank...so he can share his personal story and his mission with you in person. It may be at the end of the first week or it could be a few weeks later after you have had the chance to experience Happy State Bank.

Time with Pat is a critical part of the on-boarding process, and it typically takes a couple of hours. You learn how the bank began, how the mission was created, and how that mission is carried out, day after day.

I sat in on many meetings at Happy State Bank—a bank officers' meeting, a monthly board meeting, an annual stockholders meeting, an annual employee party, and impromptu meetings. Everything discussed was in line with protecting and perpetuating the culture that had been built from their belief system, valuing people, knowing what they can control, their mission, and non-negotiables.

Happy State Bank's belief system, mission, and 20 absolute core values—non-negotiables—are inseparable. "We cover everything that's on the list," he told me about their meetings, "but we do it by talking about the mission."

That's no coincidence. Each and every non-negotiable on the bank's list fits the mission perfectly, which in turn fits his belief system perfectly. They are built upon knowing what they can control. And valuing people is always at the base of everything they do. All five work together. If you want to work at Happy State Bank, you've got to buy in to all five—no ifs, ands, or buts!

I asked Pat to tell me about a time when someone he'd hired had failed to buy in. Pat told me about a senior management hire who had given all the right answers and asked all the right questions during the interview process. All the references had checked out. But it soon became apparent that the part about honoring the Golden Rule in his interactions with co-owners was not coming naturally to him.

"He was having trouble adjusting," Pat told me. "He wasn't used to working the way we work here, and we can usually spot that within 60 days, definitely within 90 days. We started talking to him at 90 days. When we got to 120 days and we could see that his style of interacting with other co-owners was still an issue, we said to him, 'OK, how do you want to handle this? Do you want to resign, or do we just write down that we fired you?' He opted for a graceful exit."

As Renee McNeely, Happy's Vice President and Human Resource Director, put it, "If they don't fit the culture, we allow them to go somewhere else."

How do you align with your present company? Does it reflect your beliefs and mission? How would you know if you don't know what you believe?

> **The whole power of a non-negotiable arises from its being a standard that you take on and live in your personal life first and then extend into your business life. It's not the other way around.**

It's OK if your beliefs and mission don't align with your company—although you might not want to stay there long term. You probably shouldn't work somewhere your beliefs are suppressed. People flourish when they are free to be themselves and are valued for that. We all flourish in a non-judgmental environment. The point is to know what you believe—and why. It's perfectly acceptable for your beliefs to be birthed out of inspired standards—and for that to affect your personal life and corporate life positively.

Pat Hickman has built a culture where everyone is expected to speak up and share new ideas. (You'll see this later in the book in detail.) He values people—and all they can bring to the table. He has a foundational understanding of people and how they are the ones who have grown the organization. He talks about people and the bank in the same breath—always. He's loyal to his people, and they are loyal to him. He wants innovation and progress—but he expects any ideas that are implemented to complement the culture that's been built on the belief system, valuing people, knowing what you can control, the mission, and non-negotiables for Happy State Bank.

8

DEVELOPING YOUR
NON-NEGOTIABLES

By the time you finish reading this book, I hope your thinking will have been expanded, but more importantly, your understanding. When we understand something, transformation has the potential to occur. Pat has successfully communicated so that his employees understand and daily implement 20 non-negotiables. They are the core of how he leads Happy State Bank—or, to be more accurate, how he supports the culture that runs the bank. Remember, Drayton McLane said it is Pat's job to preserve the culture, and we defined culture as a shared belief that expresses itself in action.

Remember the definition of a non-negotiable? A positive standard that respects the rights of others and is absolute. Happy State Bank's list of 20 non-negotiables are all *expressions* of the mission, which is in turn an *expression* of Pat's personal belief system. They all line up. That's why Pat would not knowingly jeopardize any of the 20 items on his list. They are each locked in too tightly to his personal beliefs and his personal mission.

I can tell you from personal experience that I have never seen him choose to back down on any of these 20 absolutes! I think his employees, customers, and stakeholders will tell you the same thing. With Pat, everything points in the same direction. Together, his beliefs, mission, and non-negotiables deliver authenticity—the unmistakable feeling you get when someone is believing, speaking, and acting consistently.

I realized, before I had spent much time on this project, that it was the passion with which Pat lays out Happy State Bank's non-negotiables, and then sticks to them, that drew me to him that first day in Amarillo. It wasn't a spell. His commitment to his non-negotiables was what made me and everyone else in the room want to support him and be associated with him—regardless of whether he and I agreed on every single item on his list. Within just a few minutes, he inspired us all with his personal sense of purpose.

NON-NEGOTIABLES ARE A POWERFUL WEAPON

The sense of being around someone who is authentic and lives his or her own non-negotiables is magnetic. This is how the most inspiring people attract others—employees, customers, stakeholders, friends, you name it. When they are coupled with action—actions in defense of non-negotiables—they tell other people exactly who you are.

To be clear, there is a difference between just saying you have non-negotiables and living them. The minute you have the opportunity to live a non-negotiable and you don't do so, it stops being a non-negotiable. If you don't do it, you're a liar. You have to think twice and then twice again before you let a non-negotiable slip. If it slips, there will be a loss of credibility from the people around you, and it is hard to get a non-negotiable back once you've let it go. The minute you *do* live a non-negotiable, you tap in to a deep source of personal and organizational power. Non-negotiables always work on every level—from home to the office.

In the marketplace, non-negotiables are your ultimate weapon. The best example I know of happens to involve the banking industry—and Happy State Bank. Here are graphics that show how Happy State Bank performed during the seven-year period that included the global financial crisis (2006-2012), as compared with the rest of the industry.

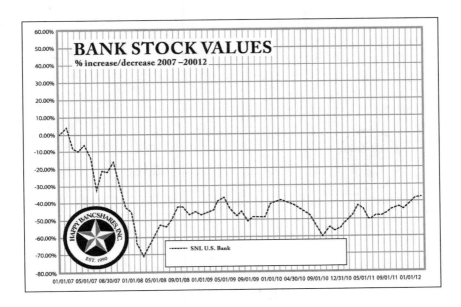

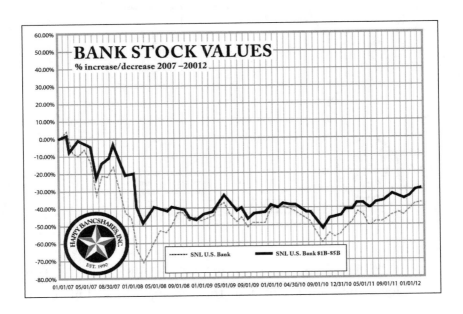

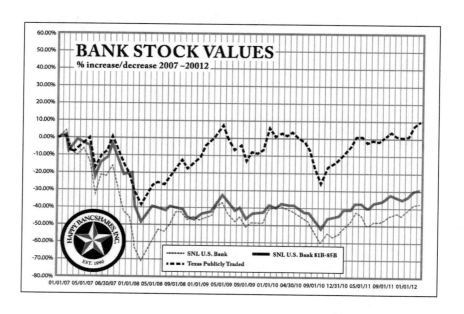

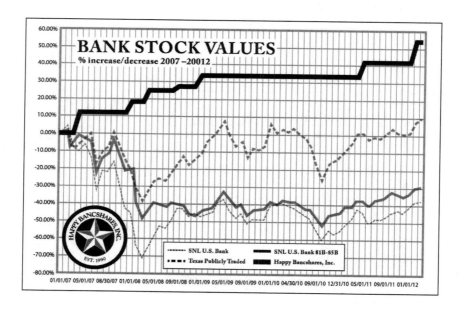

Happy State Bank's line doesn't parallel the industry's ebb and flow—they outperformed their competitors, but more importantly, they didn't even fluctuate at all with the rest of the industry. Happy State Bank doesn't let the competition and economy dictate their results—their non-negotiables do! What makes Pat's bank different than all the other banks that dealt with the global financial crisis of this period? It had non-negotiables in place—something much of the rest of the industry didn't have! If that fact doesn't make you want to learn more about harnessing the power of non-negotiables, I don't know what will.

It's OK not to know what your own belief system, your own mission, your own non-negotiables are right now. There's plenty of time to figure all of that out. What I want to make sure you understand right now, though, is that stating non-negotiables and then failing to live them is where both people and organizations run into trouble. Notice that a whole lot of banks made a whole lot of noise about "sound lending practices" and "ethical business practices" in the period leading up to 2008—but didn't exactly live up to those standards. Happy State Bank did—and the difference is evident.

NON-NEGOTIABLES LEAD TO ACCOUNTABILITY

Knowing and living your non-negotiables is not just about building a good business. It's first and foremost about living a good life by being fully accountable to others. This brings me to a key point. Because Pat has made a non-negotiable that says, "Do what's right," people who learn this and interact with him know they can depend on that commitment.

When Pat gives his word to someone, a powerful change in chemistry happens between Pat and the other person. The quality of the relationship improves to a much higher level compared to what it would have been like if Pat didn't have this particular non-negotiable—all because Pat has taken on personal accountability in that relationship for doing what he knows to be right. Pat is a master at relationships. When I saw this happening, I realized that Pat had grasped intuitively the difference between responsibility and accountability. We are responsible for things, but we are accountable to people. We are accountable when we make a clear commitment to one or more people. We can't be accountable to a thing. A report is not going to hold us accountable, but a person can.

We are responsible for things, but we are accountable to people. We are accountable when we make a clear commitment to one or more people. We can't be accountable to a thing. A report is not going to hold us accountable. We can only be accountable to a person.

It takes practice to learn how to honor accountability—how to live an accountable life. That's because accountability is not easy. Accountability is about a way of thinking. Accountability is about personal choices, feelings, attitudes, relationships, and beliefs. It is the natural outcome of knowing your beliefs, valuing people, knowing what you can control, your mission, and what is non-negotiable in your life—and living them. Knowing what those five components are in your life takes sustained effort over time—but the quality of life they produce is worth it.

Pat's example reminds me that our *actions* around accountability must expand if we are going to expand our Accountability Zone™. That's why I'm writing this book—to inspire you to expand the actions you are willing to take around accountability, just as Pat inspired me.

THREE QUESTIONS TO ASK YOURSELF

Most people think they are living up to the standard of accountability, or something close to it, but they aren't. Not really. It was as a direct result of meeting Pat Hickman and studying his example that I formulated the following account-ability questions, which show exactly what the standard for personal accountability really is. When it comes to accountability, there are three questions we all have to answer.

The first question is: Do you really want to be accountable?

The question isn't: Do you want to be accountable? The word *really* is critical. On the surface, the immediate answer would seem to be, "Yes." But many, many people who say, "Yes," in answer to this question do not *really* carry out *actions* that are in alignment with accountability to other people. You can tell exactly what a person believes by observing their actions. My father must have told me a million times, "Actions speak louder than words!" A lot of people don't like talking about direct personal accountability, about whether or not they *really* have non-negotiables in their relationships with other people, because they simply don't want to be held accountable.

The second question is: Do you value people?

And by "value people," I mean tall people, short people, fat people, skinny people, rich people, poor people, black people, white people, other-colored people, people who live in houses, people who live on the street, people who are your customers, people who aren't your customers, people who share your belief system, people who don't, people who have a different religious or cultural background than you do—everyone.

So: Do you value people? Are you equally invested in being accountable to the people in your organization or life regardless of what they can offer you? When you value people, you realize that all people have value, all people have something to give, all people have knowledge to share, all people have perspectives and insights you can learn from. All people have value.

The third question is: Whom do you serve?

Lots of people take action, but not everyone takes action with the clear purpose of serving other people. Do your actions serve yourself and your ego, or do you serve others? True leadership is always about serving others. It's a concerted effort to support the people around you by understanding what their needs and goals are—and helping them to fulfill those needs and achieve those goals. That doesn't mean we shouldn't be taking care of our own needs and goals. What it does mean is that we see serving others as a win-win. When we serve the people around us, and we help them to be successful, what ultimately happens is that we become more successful at the same time.

Many times in an organization or on a team, someone will withhold information so they can present those facts at the next meeting with the boss. Why? That person wants to look good. Everything is about their ego and their perceived best path to advancement. When your actions serve others, you provide them with the information as it arises, because you know it may be of value to them in their efforts now. At an upcoming meeting with the boss they may share that information before you do, but that doesn't matter to you. You have a larger purpose—honoring your non-negotiables and doing what's right. And anyway, if you share the information and serve as many people as possible, most of them will probably be singing your praises! Withholding information is self-serving. Sharing information that could be of value to others is serving other people. When you look to serve other people you are looking to be accountable.

Our own sense of purpose is not an accident. It happens while we're taking actions that serve others. That's when the most meaningful successes we can achieve in life happen, too.

It is only when we really want to be accountable to people and our actions support that, only when we truly value people, only when we look to serve first, that the truly great things happen in our lives. True accountability depends on all three of these areas being aligned, all of the time. Pat excels at this special kind of leadership because it is rooted in non-negotiables.

Here's the thing about non-negotiables, though: They only work if you adopt them 24/7. If you imagine you can have one set of standards for your personal life but another set of standards in your business life, then you haven't yet grasped what a non-negotiable really is.

Your non-negotiables define you as an individual. They determine who you are, what you believe, and how you choose to interact with the world around you—not just sometimes, but all the time. That's where non-negotiables really come from—you. Non-negotiables are not really about other people. They are about where *you* are, where *you* stand. Your non-negotiables may attract others, but that's only a secondary issue. First and foremost, your non-negotiables must say, "This is who I am, no matter what."

NON-NEGOTIABLES ARE
ABSOLUTE STANDARDS

The whole power of a non-negotiable arises from its being a standard that you take on and live in your personal life *first*, and then extend into your business life. It's not the other way around. It's a standard by which you measure every decision—and never waver. I've observed people who maintain the highest standards of integrity, like Pat, and those who vacillate and aren't the same at the dinner table and the board table—and the difference is evident in their success. The difference is evident in their relationships as well.

Whenever we decide something is an absolute in our life and then live it as a non-negotiable, we control that aspect of our life.

Even when we use universal terms like "standards" and "commitments," people still interpret them differently. To help us understand the true meaning I'm conveying, consider the following three levels of commitment to our standards.

The lowest level of commitment to our standards is the opinion.

For instance, consider the commitment we've been discussing: "Do what's right." We could also say, "I do what's right." We could phrase it in any number of ways. But no matter how we choose to say it, at the lowest level, we don't yet have any action to serve as evidence that we mean it. It's all talk. There has been only verbal expression without any tangible action on our part in support of the opinion that we've shared. We haven't yet *done* anything in support of the value. As a result, we have not yet set a non-negotiable.

The next level of commitment to our standards is the action.

At this level, we have taken some kind of conscious action, however small, in support of keeping our word. So if we have done what's right, on purpose, even one single time, then we have moved up to this second level. It's not just an opinion anymore. We can defend our opinion based on evidence. The trouble is, our actions usually aren't consistent. That is, we may not take actions that support our word all the time. For instance, we may only support our words with actions when it is easy or popular to do so. We still haven't identified a non-negotiable.

The third level of commitment to our standards is the non-negotiable.

At this level, we made a decision to *take a stand* in support of our opinion and our belief, even though it might be easier to do something else. In other words, we hold the line when it's unpopular or difficult to do so. We take a stand and make the standard, "Do what's right," as something that is unyielding in our life. It's something internal, something we own, an outcome we can and do control. Whenever we decide something is an *absolute* in our life and then live it as a non-negotiable, we control that aspect of our life.

Pop Quiz: You are getting ready to jump out of a plane, and you have three parachutes to choose from. Would you pick the one that had been packed by someone for whom "Safety

First" was an *opinion*? The one that had been packed by a person who *occasionally took action* on the principle that safety comes first? Or the person who had consistently made "Safety First" a non-negotiable condition of his or her life?

NORTH IS NORTH

At the level of the non-negotiable, everything becomes a whole lot clearer. Non-negotiables are like a compass, and north is always north. What makes any decision a non-negotiable is the fact that you adhere to the right direction, not just sometimes, but all the time. Once made, the non-negotiable is not open for discussion. Once you know where true north is, and you never vary from that direction, you can be truly accountable to yourself and others.

> The sense of being around someone who is authentic and lives his or her own non-negotiables is magnetic. When they are coupled with action—actions in defense of non-negotiables—they tell other people exactly who you are.

At the third level of commitment to your standards, there is no longer any question about whether someone "made" you not do what you knew to be right, or whether something "justified" you in making an exception when you didn't follow your gut about what was right. You're the person behind the wheel. No one else. You are either headed north, in alignment with your own non-negotiable, or you're not. And if you're not, and your non-negotiable ever slips, then you know who has to change direction and resume control of the journey.

Even with a great excuse, an opinion or an action is not the same as a non-negotiable. An opinion or an action only becomes a non-negotiable once we actually take a stand for it *when it would be easier not to.* Just talking about the standard is not enough.

BUILDING A NON-NEGOTIABLE BY BUILDING PERSONAL ACCOUNTABILITY

Doing what's right is a non-negotiable for Pat Hickman. Once Pat gives his word on something, he will not consciously choose to go against that word because keeping your word with someone is what is right. It's an absolute for him. Do what's right. That's a non-negotiable, an absolute for Pat. It's a personal standard that extends into every aspect of everything he does. It's something he operates and lives by, 24/7, no matter what.

But it wasn't always like that. In Chapter 2, I shared his story of how he and his investors negotiated buying Happy State Bank from Carl Small. Pat is a human being like the rest of us. He had to *work his way up* to that point where doing what's right was not just an opinion, but a non-negotiable component of who he really is as an individual. It's something he now controls. But Pat got to this place—beginning with that painful experience with Carl Small—by turning his own *opinions and actions* about doing what's right into a *non-negotiable.*

You'll recall the final deal on buying Happy State Bank cost Pat and his investors an extra $100,000. But because that experience birthed Pat's first non-negotiable, he knows it was the best $100,000 he ever spent. It taught him how to have predetermined non-negotiables that are applicable to all of life and its decisions.

You have to know what you believe. That is where it always starts. You really can identify, reinforce, and take a stand for your own beliefs; learn what you can control; value people; define a mission; and develop them into non-negotiables. Again, my aim is not to get you to take on the exact same non-negotiables that Pat has or I have. My aim is to help you identify and strengthen your own non-negotiables. That's how you determine who you really are as an individual—and unlock the freedom of control they afford, positive control that moves your life forward.

To this day, whenever I say the words "Happy State Bank," people smile and chuckle. Then, when they learn about how well the bank is doing, they want to know: "Is it just because of the name, or is there more to it than that?"

There's more to it than that—a lot more. To learn *why* Happy State Bank is doing as well as it is, and why Pat's personal leadership is such a great example for all of us on both the personal and the organizational level, we need to take a close look at all of the bank's non-negotiables. Keep reading and we'll go through each and every one.

PART THREE

HAPPY STATE BANK'S 20 NON-NEGOTIABLES

9

THE LIST EVERYONE KNOWS

As we look in depth at Pat's 20 non-negotiables for Happy State Bank, notice that in each case we are looking at something that Pat himself *practices*. It's also important to know that although Pat did put these in writing, he had several people help edit them. Pat will always tell you his board and officers are invaluable—and that he is surrounded by great people.

NON-NEGOTIABLE #1:
DO WHAT'S RIGHT

Years ago, a nervous-looking young couple walked into a tiny bank in Canyon, Texas—a small town just south of Amarillo and home to the Palo Duro Canyon. They wanted to talk about taking out a personal loan.

The bank had only been open for about six months. That bank had, as a practical matter, approximately zero market share. Hardly anyone had ever heard of it.

It had opened up right in the middle of the big savings and loan crisis that decimated much of the nation's financial sector. You may remember the savings and loan crisis of the '80s and '90s. The scorecard looked like this: 747 failed financial institutions, and a tab to the FDIC and ultimately the surviving banks of $87.9 billion.

This little bank opened its doors right after that disaster, in a state that had been hit particularly hard.

The husband and wife who walked in through the doors of that bank did so at about ten in the morning. They each looked concerned, and perhaps even a little desperate. They scanned the room for someone to help them, but they saw that the only loan officer on duty was busy with another customer. As it happened, though, the president of the bank was free.

He walked toward them. He greeted the couple, introduced himself, shook hands, and asked how he could help.

The husband told the bank president his name and his wife's name, then he said they wanted to borrow six thousand dollars.

The bank president smiled and said he'd be happy to walk them through the process of applying for the loan. He escorted them into his office, asked them to take a seat, got out the paperwork they needed, and began to fill in the blanks with them. He got a little information about their background, their income, and their ties to their community. But the bank president couldn't help noticing that the couple seemed fidgety.

Something was wrong. The husband and wife kept looking at each other, kept looking at the clock on the wall, kept forcing themselves to look back at the paperwork they were supposed to be filling out. There was no other word for it: They were distracted. They acted like their minds were somewhere else.

This unusual behavior kept up for a few minutes, until finally, the president of the bank said, in a kindly way, "You all seem kind of nervous. Is there anything you want to tell me about what's going on in your world today?"

The husband sighed, then looked at the wife. The wife nodded. The husband looked at the bank president, and then said: "We've been trying to adopt a baby for a long time."

The bank president nodded, and then he looked over at the wife. He noticed that she was starting to cry.

The husband explained, "The bank down the street told us they would loan us the money to pay the adoption fee," he said, his voice shaky. "We went down there this morning to get the money, and they told us they wouldn't be able to loan it to us. It turns out we had a problem on our credit report. We paid the money back, but that doesn't matter now. We paid it late. We got turned down for the loan. If we don't get to Fort Worth (Texas) to pick up that baby this afternoon, we lose him." (It's important to know here that the drive from Canyon to Fort Worth is more than five hours.)

> **Pat constantly asks himself: What's the right thing to do here? Not only that: He has built a company whose employees ask themselves the same thing—all day long!**

The bank president looked stunned. He stared at the couple, then he took a deep breath. He looked at the papers on his desk, and said: "Oh, my gosh, why in the world are we wasting time worrying about this stupid application?"

In an instant he was up out of his seat.

He brought the couple out of his office and started walking them back toward the front of the bank. "Come on out here so we can get you a cashier's check."

Briskly, but politely, he started a teller on that task.

He asked them to whom the cashier's check should be made out. He passed that information on to the teller.

He told the couple that he trusted them. He knew damn well they were good for the money. He asked if they had a good car for the drive to Fort Worth, which they did. He was glad about that. He wanted them on the road, headed for their appointment, not wasting time with him in Canyon. He would see them tomorrow, and they could finish up the paperwork then.

"Here's your cashier's check," he said, handing it over to them.

They were beaming. The wife still had tears in her eyes, but now they were a different kind of tears.

"Now you two listen," the bank president said, "I want you to drive fast but drive carefully. Don't you have a wreck going or coming, because I've still got to have you sign the note for this loan. You can get back up here tomorrow. But right now, you have got to get out of here and point that car toward Fort Worth so you can *go get that baby!*"

The husband and wife were *both* crying by now.

They shook his hand. They took the check. And then they were gone.

The next day, they showed up at the bank holding a baby.

The wife said, "We want you to know, we are coming here to show off this baby to you and the rest of the people at the bank first. We haven't even shown him to the grandparents yet."

Two decades later, they are still customers of that bank. That bank president was J. Pat Hickman.

One of Pat's non-negotiables for Happy State Bank was—and is—"Do what's right."

You might have been thinking, as you read this story, that Pat was breaking every rule in the bank when he loaned that couple that $6,000 without any paperwork. But you would be wrong. He wasn't breaking *every* rule.

He might have been breaking a lot of *little* rules, but he was honoring the *big* rule, the rule that matters enough to be a non-negotiable for Pat, and for his bank: Do what you know is right.

In service of this non-negotiable, Pat constantly asks himself: What's the right thing to do here? Not only that, he has built a company whose employees ask themselves the same thing—all day long!

Once when the bank was switching over an acquisition to the Happy computer system, there were a few problems with some customers' debit cards from the old bank. A customer who had been grocery shopping at Walmart called the bank and told them that her card wasn't working. Most banks would have apologized for the problem, explained that the system was still being worked on, and assured her that the problem would be resolved just as soon as possible. But when you work at Happy, you ask, "What's the right thing to do here?" And the teller who took that call knew that leaving that customer stranded at the checkout line was not the right thing to do.

The lady who took the call knew that customer had just spent an hour filling her shopping cart with the groceries her family needed for the week. She knew from her own personal experience how time consuming that can be, and how aggravating it was to hit an obstacle of any kind once you got to the point where you swipe your card. While she was still on the line with the customer, the teller found out how much the amount due was—and debited the customer's account for that amount. Then she asked the customer where she was, took the money out of the cash drawer, and drove to Walmart to meet the customer in person—and pay for those groceries in cash!

That was the right thing to do.

Happy State Bank is accountable to its customers for honoring the Golden Rule—because Pat Hickman is. And make no mistake, he really does strive to honor the Golden Rule with everyone with whom he comes in contact!

"Do unto others as you would have them do unto you." Pat Hickman's bank proves that really is a viable business success strategy. It is a viable strategy for success in life, as well. And if you're on board with what I have shared so far, I am assuming it is a viable strategy for *you*.

NON-NEGOTIABLE #2:
ATTITUDE IS EVERYTHING

"I've fired a whole lot more people for not having the right attitude than for not having the right skills," Pat told me one day.

That remark came my way very early on in our relationship. It transformed the way I thought about Happy State Bank.

At first, I thought it might have been hyperbole, that he might have been exaggerating in order to impress me, that—like a lot of corporate leaders—Pat might be trying to send a message to his people with tough talk that didn't actually translate into pink slips.

No.

I was able to confirm, in multiple discussions with multiple employees at all levels of the bank, that Pat really did mean this. He really did fire people—lots of them—for the sole reason that they consistently brought to the workplace the prevailing attitude that most of us either tolerate or put up with in our work and our life—the attitude of indifference, of cynicism, of jadedness.

> **If you want to work here, that means you want to give people your heart, not just your words or actions. Our co-owners and our customers can see through poor and lousy attitudes, and they can see through insincerity. A good attitude is OK, but a great attitude is what we expect.**

I had undeniable third-party confirmation on this: Maintaining a jaded attitude at Happy State Bank really is a fireable offense. No kidding! Of course, that's not to say that, if you come from a place where a different attitude is the norm, or if you're going through a tough spot in your life, you get fired for having a bad day. There's a grace period, particularly in the situation where someone is "transitioning" from a workplace that doesn't share Happy State Bank's non-negotiables. You get some time to adopt the right attitude toward your peers, your customers, and your stakeholders. But if that time goes by and you're still habitually indifferent, cynical, and jaded when you walk into work in the morning, you're history.

When Pat speaks to new employees he touches on this non-negotiable early and often. Here's what he says to back it up:

"Life is 10 percent what happens to you and 90 percent your attitude toward it. So your attitude is always on display. Most people don't get that. Here, we get that. See, if you want to work here, that means you want to give people your heart, not just your words or actions. Our co-owners and our customers can see through poor and lousy attitudes, and they can see through insincerity. A good attitude is OK, but a great attitude is what we expect. So I urge you not to let good take the place of great. If you want to work here, I really do want you to be the best person you can possibly be, every hour of the working day. That's the standard."

Pat told me that he often gives a variation on this speech to people who don't work at Happy State Bank. He said, "I love talking about attitude to people outside the bank. People come up to me afterward and say, 'You know that part you said about firing people who don't have the right attitude? My boss needs to hear that!' I have personally experienced many times after letting someone go, the people who used to work with that person say, 'I wish you had let so-and-so go a lot sooner.'"

I'll tell you a secret: Good people are *drawn* to this non-negotiable, not frightened by it! They don't want to work with people who have lousy attitudes. They *want* the boss to take a stand on *attitude is everything.*

NON-NEGOTIABLE #3:
SERVICE IS THE GOAL

Pat told me: "I want people who will go the extra mile, who will bend over backward, who will give 100 percent. So I know that's what we have to do with our own people.

"Think about it. Our standard is that we always greet our customers with a smile. And our standard is that we always call customers by name. After all, the sweetest sounding word in anyone's ear is the sound of their own name. Well, how can we get the people behind the counter to do that with the customers if we don't first do it with them? We have to serve them first. That's why we smile, and use people's names, and call them co-owners, not employees. That's what they are. Co-owners in this experience of service.

"There's a Bible verse about the servant's heart: *'But it shall not be so among you. Whoever would be great among you must be your servant, and whoever would be first among you must be slave of all.'* That's the way we run this bank. That's how we try to treat each other. And that's how we try to treat our customers."

(The verse Pat quoted, I later found out, was Mark 10:43-44.)

Pat shared that he loves the examples set by Chick-Fil-A® and Southwest Airlines: "They really get great service along with a great service/product."

We really do try to treat every customer as if they had $1 million in the bank. I realize we may differentiate in the rates we pay or charge, but we should never differentiate on the quality of our service.

Pat had firsthand experience with the service that Herb Kelleher, former CEO of Southwest Airlines, personally offered. "I used to travel all over the state when I was the Chairman of the Independent Bankers Association of Texas. I flew from San Antonio to Dallas on many occasions. Herb Kelleher lives in San Antonio. He would commute to Love Field in Dallas every morning and back again in the evening. I was on that morning flight several times. Herb was always greeting people at the door, assisting in the boarding process and even serving people once on board. He was a great example for me.

"And yes, we really do try to treat every customer as if they had $1 million in the bank. I realize we may differentiate in the rates we pay or charge, but we should never differentiate on the quality of our service. And when we say service is the goal, what we mean is that we empower our co-owners to take care of our customers. It's that simple.

"So, if you work here, your job is to not let the customers leave without a smile on their face.

"Your job is to do what is best for the customer, and sometimes that is not what is most profitable for the bank. Our goal is to develop long-term relationships with our customers, not make a short-term profit on them.

"If you work here, your job is to sincerely care about that individual customer.

"People only talk about two kinds of service: Off-the-chart, really great service, *or* really super-bad service—and I want people to talk about us.

"When it comes right down to it, great customer service is our only advantage over our competition. So we like co-owners who are consumed with service and who maintain a servant's heart. We know we have to serve *each other*, every day, in order to create and sustain that happy experience."

This non-negotiable is the Golden Rule in action. A great example of the level of service I'm talking about is the way Happy State Bank handles "operating hours." Although the lobby of each Happy State branch technically "opens" at 9 a.m. and "closes" at 4 p.m.—in that those are the posted hours of operation—the doors are unlocked 15 minutes early and stay unlocked, and the employees stay there to serve you for another half hour beyond the official closing time!

When I asked Pat why he did business that way, he asked, "Have you ever tried to get to the bank by 4 p.m., and gotten there at 4:05 p.m., and found the doors locked and the place empty?"

I said, "Sure."

He said, "How did that make you feel?"

I said, "Lousy—even though I knew it was my fault I was late."

He said, "We don't want people to feel that way."

Relax!

When people are relaxed, they're able to serve the customer at a whole different level. I talked to plenty of Happy State Bank customers who told me that they had worked with someone within that branch back when it had been owned by a larger national chain. I always asked the customer: "What's the difference between working with that person now and working with that person when the big national bank was in charge?"

And the answer was always the same. It was some variation on: "He/she is so much more relaxed!"

That relaxation is a conscious choice, a part of the culture of mutual service at Happy State Bank. People are there for each other. They can relax. That's the result of the Servant's Heart philosophy that Pat talks about. I mentioned, during one of our interviews, that it seemed like the exact opposite of the philosophy of the big banks he competes against.

"I don't know whether what the big banks are doing makes sense for them or not in terms of customer service," Pat replied. "In fact, I don't really care what they're doing, and I don't care how they're doing it. I care about this bank, these people, these customers, this market. That's really all I focus on. I don't worry that much about the competition, to tell you the truth. All I can tell you is what works for us. And I know that if you hire good people and take care of them and give them the freedom they need to take care of other people, then they can relax and get to work.

"So we try to serve our own people first, so that they can serve the customer. We do that in a lot of ways. For instance, by encouraging them to do their very best, and saying, 'Rise to be a better person,' and then getting out of their way. And you know what? They respond.

"When someone says that to you, 'Rise to be a better person, show us what kind of service you can give,' then something really powerful happens to you. You go home, you look yourself in the mirror, and you decide that you want to make a difference. And that's what we mean when we say *service is the goal*. It's about making a difference.

"We are out to create a servant's heart at all levels of this bank. We are out to serve our co-owners and, through them, our customers. We are out to give each and every one of our people the freedom and the resources they need to rise to be a better person…so they can personally make a difference with each and every one of our customers."

NON-NEGOTIABLE #4: TREAT EVERY CO-OWNER AT LEAST AS WELL AS YOU TREAT YOUR BEST CUSTOMER

Notice that this non-negotiable pairs with the non-negotiable "service is *the* goal." They are really two sides of the same coin.

To understand this non-negotiable, you need to understand that everyone who works at Happy State Bank really is a co-owner of the bank, because there is a compensation system in place that uses employee stock ownership. That's why Pat refers to everyone who works at the bank—including himself—as a co-owner. They really are co-owners. However, what's much more important than how people are compensated, or what they are called, is how they are treated. And that's what this non-negotiable is all about.

Take a moment to look at the implications of this non-negotiable very closely. What this one is saying is that *every* co-owner (regardless of job title) is obliged to treat *every* other co-owner not just as a respected colleague, but as though he or she were the most valued patron of the bank.

That's a very high standard!

Following it means there is no room for pulling rank, no room for gossip or backbiting, no room for mind games or rivalries in *any* relationship with *anyone* with whom you work. If you want to work at Happy State Bank, then you agree to treat everyone on the team, regardless of position, with the same total respect and authentic personal concern you would show to the bank's most important customer.

Most companies don't even come close to meeting this standard. Yet there are no exceptions to this for anyone working at Happy State Bank.

> "We are all on the same team. We are working for the same goals. That means we have to start from the assumption that everyone is giving his or her best. We don't start from the assumption that someone is having a problem. We have to give each other the benefit of the doubt, just as we have to give our customers the benefit of the doubt."
>
> —PAT

Why? Well, think of it this way. How can you and I deliver superior customer service if we're consistently gossiping about each other, or resenting each other, or sabotaging each other during the work day? We can't.

We can't possibly be in a great frame of mind for our customer if our relationship with each other is in trouble. That's why this is a non-negotiable. We have to be in a great frame of mind with the people we work with every day, no matter what the job titles in question are, if we really expect to deliver outstanding service to our customers.

Now, this particular non-negotiable brings us to one of Pat's most remarkable personal traits. Unlike so many of the corporate leaders out there, Pat really does model this standard, day in and day out.

I have seen proof of this with my own eyes and heard it with my own ears. He treats his senior management team just as well as he treats his best customer. Not only that, he treats the *brand-new hire* as well as he treats his best customer—and everyone in between.

Let me repeat: It is just as easy for the brand new hire to have a conversation with Pat, and be heard, as it is for someone in his inner circle of senior executives to have a conversation, and be heard. How many corporate leaders can honestly make that claim?

Why does Pat do it? In discussions with me about this non-negotiable, Pat emphasized to me over and over again that the only way this standard can possibly prevail in any organization is if people see the person at the top living it on a daily basis.

That's true of every non-negotiable discussed in this book, but it's worth noting here that Pat really does make this a personal priority, day in and day out, with everyone he encounters in his organization. For my part, I have to tell you that I have never met a CEO or company founder who executes on this principle with the same consistency and integrity that Pat does.

Pat told me: "We are all on the same team. We are working for the same goals. That means we have to start from the assumption that everyone is giving his or her best. We don't start from the assumption that someone is having a problem. We have to give each other the benefit of the doubt, just as we have to give our customers the benefit of the doubt.

"And I realize it starts with me. I want to bring out the best in every co-owner. I want them to go the extra mile. I want everyone to create a happy experience for every other co-owner. So I do that for everyone I come in contact with here.

"It's just nice to work with nice people. But it doesn't happen by accident. It has to start at the top. I don't care what it is: It could be a Boy Scout troop, or a football team, or a church, or a business. People take on the personality of the person who's sitting at the top. So you've got to drink your own Kool-Aid, and then you've got to surround yourself with people who drink it, too. That's the only way this works.

"I'm a real believer in the principle that the vast majority of people really do want to be nice. They really do want to be productive. They really do want to do the right thing, and if you put them into an environment that allows them to do that and prosper—stand back. Not only are they going to excel. They are going to start telling people, 'Hey, this is a great place to work.' And that's what you want. But it has to start at the top."

> **The people in any organization have to experience someone actually taking a stand for a non-negotiable in a memorable way to even notice it and consider making it part of the culture customers experience on a daily basis.**

Co-Owners Who Act Like Family

Cari Roach, Happy State Bank's Marketing Director, shared this remarkable story with me about how people at Happy State Bank treat each other: "People truly care about each other here, and I know that sounds like a cliché, so I'll tell you some of my history. My husband got sick with cancer and passed away. The year he was sick was the year I realized that this place really was family.

"People from work appeared out of nowhere and offered to mow my lawn. They showed up with food, they did chores—I can't tell you all the things they did for us, and this wasn't one time. He was sick for a year, a solid year. People showed up that whole year. The last two months, I worked from home. They went and set up all my computers at home. I know that period had to be an inconvenience for people. But I never once had to say, 'Hey, do this, do that.' People just jumped in. 'She's not here. Let's do this.' And I worked as much as I could from home, but obviously I deal with sponsorships and meeting with people, so there were some things that could have fallen through the cracks. They covered for me. They brought work to me. Once a week I had a meeting and then I turned right around and brought all the work back to my home, so I didn't have to leave my husband. My coworkers truly cared for me—just like family.

"It's just the most incredible experience to have a group of people look after you the way they all looked after me. And Pat never docked me one penny in pay, ever, regardless of what the sick policy said. It just wasn't counted. At one point, when things had gotten bad, I had said to Pat, 'I think I'm not as comfortable as I was, leaving him alone this much. He's fallen a time or two.' All Pat said was, 'Go. Stay with him.' There were no questions asked. And I had only been there two and a half years at that point. The caring is from the top down. So if you want to ask me whether I'm loyal to this company, my answer is, 'You can only imagine,' because I've seen firsthand how this kind of thing plays out at other companies—not like what happened here, not like what happened to me.

"When he (my husband) passed, so many came to the funeral. They shut the bank down! It was just a priority. People drove from all the outlying areas (where we have branches). You can tell people cared.

"In contrast, when I was at a large bank—before coming to work at Happy State Bank—I had to tell our supervisor whose husband was diagnosed with cancer and was sick about a year, 'You can only be gone this many days and you're out of sick leave.'

"She was leaving her husband alone when he shouldn't have been left alone, because there was no money. She was out of sick leave and her pay would have been docked.

"The bank did nothing. The management did nothing. The community had garage sales. We all gave money. We supported to help pay her bills just within ourselves. The bank did not support that or do anything to support that. That wouldn't happen here (at Happy State Bank).

"When my husband got sick, he couldn't work anymore. We lost a whole income and didn't get disability. Social Security takes a while. You apply for it in a month and it can take up to two years to get approval for disability because he was not eligible. But if your life expectancy is less than a year, they'll rush it.

We applied in January, and he died in June. We never got a dime; he had paid all his life.

"I came to work one day (after he had passed) and it was our daughter's last semester of college. She had lots of expenses, and there on my desk was a check for five thousand dollars."

The money was from the "For Happy's Sake" fund sponsored by employees to help other employees during difficult times. It's another way the Happy State Bank family helps each other.

"Not only is it the people, the bank, working from home, no cut in pay, losing one income...but it's the whole package," Cari went on to explain. "The emotional support, the physical support, the financial support. That's caring for your people."

"For Happy's Sake"

This powerful story—which literally brought tears to my eyes when I heard it from Cari—mentions the fund named "For Happy's Sake." Pat told me how this fund began. It's one more story of how Happy's co-owners reflect the culture.

"Debbie Gray runs our operations department," Pat said. "Years ago, her husband borrowed money from us to open a restaurant. Not long after that, he was diagnosed with terminal cancer. He had an SBA (Small Business Administration) loan, and when his interest payment came due, he couldn't pay it. Debbie didn't have the money either. So I went to the board.

"'Guys, I want to bonus something. I want to do something.'

"Each of my directors, which I think was 14 at the time, personally wrote Debbie a check for $1,000, as a gift, so she didn't have to pay taxes on it. It began with a motion, a second, and a unanimous decision. And yet it wasn't 'bank business,' meaning it was a decision funded by personal gifts, not bank money.

"Debbie's husband passed away several months later, and she received a large sum from an insurance policy. She came to us and said, 'Pat, I want to pay back all the directors.'

"Well, every one of the directors said, 'You're crazy. We're not going to take that money. It's yours. Forget it.'

"Debbie turned around and wrote a check for $14,000, and we established a fund to help other employees when challenges came along outside of the ordinary. That $14,000, combined with some more our directors put in, served as seed money for what we now call 'For Happy's Sake.'

"Today, co-owners can contribute out of every paycheck if they want to. Some give $5, $2, or $10. It's their gift to their co-owners.

"We pay out anywhere from $20,000 to $40,000 a year from that fund to help co-owners. And, by the way, the bank matches whatever the co-owners contribute. We've helped people with a car payment, a house payment, or a medical bill. If there has been an extraordinary hardship, and they just need some financial help, they can get it. It's set up to where a committee reviews all the requests and extends the money. It's kept private, so even I don't know who all gets the money—just the committee members know.

"Last year, total contributions to 'For Happy's Sake' was $56,000, and we distributed $27,000. It was like $1,700 for a car repair, $2,300 toward a funeral, $1,700 total for groceries, $6,000 for medical expenses, and $10,000 for people to make their house payments. I know one story of a recipient who had to deal with their folks dying and they had to make quick travel arrangements. They couldn't afford the airline ticket, so the For Happy's Sake fund did."

Treating every co-owner at least as well as your best customer. "For Happy's Sake" is one more way the co-owners of Happy State Bank live this non-negotiable.

NON-NEGOTIABLE #5:
FAMILY FIRST

A lot of employers say they put family first. What would those two words really mean if you worked at Happy State Bank, as opposed to working somewhere else? Well, according to Pat, they mean that your family is your priority, period.

How, exactly? When, exactly?

"All the time, every time.

"So, for instance, if I were to find out that your grandpa had his 80th birthday coming up, and you knew there was a family reunion scheduled to celebrate that, and you missed it so that you could come in and be at work, you and I are going to have to have a discussion."

In other words, being at work is not an acceptable excuse for missing a family event.

Really?

Now, as an outsider, I was a little dubious at first that Pat or anyone else really would (or really could) run a company this way. I am here to tell you, though, that this really is the "rule of the road" at Happy State Bank. Whether it sounds plausible or not, whether it sounds realistic or not, whether it sounds workable or not, you really are expected to put your family first if you work here.

> **When you put family first, you get a truly committed workforce. That's because family is the reason people get up in the morning to go to work.**

I have three insights to share with you about this non-negotiable. First, I want you to understand that it's not just how Pat operates—it's how he and all of his senior executives operate, and it's also how every manager of every team operates within the bank.

Second, the reason the whole company accepts that family comes first is that Pat has repeatedly taken a stand for that. He has woven this non-negotiable into the DNA of his company for so long, with so many different people, and in so many different circumstances, it's not only become something that he's unwilling to negotiate on, it also has become something the organization refuses to negotiate.

Third, this non-negotiable doesn't exist in a vacuum. Family obligations and work obligations exist in balance at Happy State Bank, as they should at any great company. Accountability runs in both directions.

Pat told me: "I don't want to see you at work when you have a family obligation. You know why? When you put family first, you get a truly committed workforce. That's because family is the reason people get up in the morning to go to work. They do that for one reason and one reason only—to provide a better life for themselves and their families. So I tell people: 'Hey, your work will still be here tomorrow, but your family grows up.'

"There's a saying, 'No one ever died with these as his last words: I wish I had worked more.' It's true. Your family really is lots more important than this bank. So if you work here, we need you to act accordingly. More importantly, your family needs you to act accordingly."

One day, a bank teller called Pat and said, "Mr. Hickman, you lied to us in Happy Beginnings. You told us that family came first and we'd always be able to be with our family, and my boss wouldn't let me. I asked for this day off to go to my husband's granddad's birthday in Kansas and she wouldn't let me have it off."

Pat told me, "Because it was in Kansas she couldn't fly. She needed all day Friday to make the drive up for the celebration with her family on Saturday. I called the head teller and asked, 'What's the deal?'

"She said it was two things: The teller had already missed a lot of work (the head teller thought it was due to being hung over on several occasions), and two other tellers in that same branch had already asked for that same day off and she had already told them they could. She said, 'Pat we can't run the branch like that.'

"So my answer was, 'First off, if she missed that much work you should have already fired her, or at least put her on warning, and if she did it again fire her. Second, we have more than 500 people working here and you're telling me we can't find one teller to work the window? Hell, I'll come down there and work the window, but don't make me a liar. If we tell people they can have the day off, we've got to move mountains to make that happen if that's what we've gotta do. Don't ever under any circumstances go back on that one.'"

Pat really does not want to see you in the bank if you have a family commitment—a recital, birthday, anniversary, whatever. If there's a family event, and you don't show up for it, that's not cool. Now, that doesn't mean you don't have the responsibility to find someone to cover for you and to make up your work. But it does mean you know what your priorities are if you have a family member who needs you. You've got to be there for them, period. And the bank will never make you put that family member second. That's just how Pat operates, and it's how he makes sure his bank operates, too.

Here again, though, Pat will tell you this began, not just with him, but with the actions and decisions of his board.

"When we were first trying to buy the bank years ago, and we were still waiting on government approval—this was when I had quit my job and was working without a paycheck, driving to Happy from Amarillo every day—we had a total of six employees. Most of the team was well established and had grandkids, but this one woman was still young. She asked me one day, 'Pat, if you guys buy this bank, are we going to have maternity insurance?'

"I laughed and said, 'Are you kidding?! I'm married to "Fertile Myrtle" and we've got to have maternity insurance! Yeah, I know that will happen.'

"'Oh, that's so good,' she said, 'I can't wait.' And that's all she said at that point.

"Well, about three months later, we were still waiting to own the bank, and she came to me. 'Guess what,' she said, 'I'm pregnant. We don't have any health insurance yet, do we?'

"'No,' I told her, 'I'm sorry, Lisa, we don't. We don't own the bank yet, so we haven't put that into place.'

"'OK. Well, I just want you to know, I may need to borrow money or something when the baby is born.'

"Later, when we'd owned the bank three or four months, she had her baby, and there were all kinds of complications. That baby was premature and spent time in intensive care.

"So one day I asked her, 'Lisa, how much is all this going to cost you?'

"This was 1990, so if I remember right, it was around $9,000, which was insurmountable back then.

"At the next board meeting—even though we were still in this season of getting to know one another and they were watching me to see if they could trust me and follow my leadership of this bank, and we weren't making any money yet—I couldn't shake Lisa and her circumstances.

"I said, 'Guys, I know this is crazy. I know we're losing money, but we've got a young lady who was pregnant before we owned the bank, and she has no medical coverage. She's not come and asked for anything, but I feel morally like we ought to do something to let her know we care. How would all of you feel if we gave her a bonus of $1,000 to help her with her medical bills?'

"One of the directors said, 'Pat, if we do that, we'll have to hold taxes out. Would $1,000 really help?'

"'I know. It's really the thought that counts."

"Herbert Kuhlman, a rough, self-made man and cattleman spoke up. 'Well, I don't know about the rest of you boys, but that $200 a month director fee Pat has given us…I don't figure I need that for the next two months.'

"Then Harold Dillehay said, 'Herbert, if that's a motion, I'll second it.'

"I jumped on it. 'We have a motion and a second, all in favor?' It was a unanimous vote, and 12 directors gave up their little $200 fee for two months. That was $400 each and they gifted it personally to Lisa so none of it was taxed. She received $4,800 tax-free to help her through.

"Of course the employees heard about it. It reverberated throughout the whole bank. Everyone was asking, 'Did you hear what the board did for Lisa?'

"Lisa is still around today. The board set the tone from the beginning that you and your family matter. They did that—and that's still who we are today."

From the beginning, Pat and the board have led by personal example. Even when his own kids were growing up, Pat kept a pair of athletic shoes in his car, so he could swap shoes, leave work, and go out to coach or see his kids' practices and games. He never missed a game. That family commitment is a non-negotiable! So he changed shoes in the car and went to the game. If things were busy at the office (and they usually were), he may have just jumped back into his car, put his dress shoes back on again, and headed back to the office for the evening!

Actions speak louder than words! When Pat models this non-negotiable (and every one of the 20 non-negotiables), he inspires others to do the same—and so does the board of directors.

NON-NEGOTIABLE #6:
PRAYER IS OK—IT'S EVEN ENCOURAGED

To talk with Pat Hickman for more than about ten minutes is to know the power of prayer on a personal level.

Of course, I realize that these days it's a little difficult in most workplaces for people to talk openly about prayer. I realize too that there are plenty of good people out there, including many readers of this book, who prefer to operate in a world where topics like God and prayer are not discussed. I respect everyone's views on the subject, including those of the many people who believe that open, unapologetic prayer has no place in a company—or for that matter, in a book like this. I get it.

But this is a book about Happy State Bank. The act of praying to God is woven into the DNA of this organization. You cannot spend much time with anyone here without concluding that the bank is better for it.

Happy State Bank has successfully leveraged the power of prayer as a significant competitive advantage.

> **While I would never force my personal spiritual beliefs on anyone, I would also never abandon them for anyone.**
>
> **—PAT**

That is all due to Pat's example when it comes to prayer, of course. A whole lot of people follow it. Those who don't follow it respect it. I didn't run into anyone inside or outside the organization who resented it. Gary Molberg, the president of the Amarillo Chamber of Commerce, is a good friend of Pat's. He's known him for many years. Gary told me:

"One of the things you find out quickly, once you spend any amount of time talking to Pat, is that he's very open about his faith, and I admire him for that. He is a Christian and his business is Christian-based. That's just who he is. We've had ribbon cuttings for every one of his branches, and he always opens that ceremony with a prayer and he always thanks the Good Lord for everything they have. That's just how he runs his organization. He doesn't apologize for his faith. He's not afraid of it. I think that's very good. I know tons of people in the banking business, and I think Pat's emphasis on his faith is a big part of the reason why it's so different at Happy State Bank. They really are like a family over there."

Gary's reaction is typical among those who interact with Pat. People tend to admire him for putting his beliefs up front—and admire him even more for taking action on those beliefs in his own life. This is true even when the person comes from a different faith background than Christianity.

Pat operates his life and his business on a principle he calls "active dependence." It combines deep trust in God; frequently discussed, right out loud, vigorous and direct action in support of one's goals; and lots and lots of prayer—public, private, each and every day as you work to attain those goals.

Pat talks constantly about active dependence, and I asked him why during one of our interviews. He told me: "Prayer works, plain flat and simple. It's how I do business, and I don't make any excuses about that. While I would never force my personal spiritual beliefs on anyone, I would also never abandon them for anyone. My faith in my God and in his only begotten son Jesus Christ guide every decision—every one. And I don't mind talking about that."

Pat explains active dependence as follows: "If a guy needed a job, was out of work, he basically has four options in my opinion:

"One is to sit in his home all day and do nothing. If that's the case he'll never get a job.

"Two is to sit in his home and pray, nothing else, just pray. Now I'm not going to sit here and say that God won't answer that prayer, because I believe in prayer, but I've never heard of that happening. Because of my belief in prayer, I'm not going to say it's never going to happen, but I'm going to say at best it's going to take a while.

"The third way you can look for a job is the very opposite. Go out and knock on every single door in the world, leaving résumés everywhere and doing everything you can do to get that job, and in so doing you're going to get a job. My question would be, 'Is it the right job?'

"Whereas active dependence is when you actively go out looking for a job, but before you walk in that door you stop and say, 'Lord, if this is where you want me, put me here. I am depending on you. If this isn't the kind of company I need to be at, please don't let them offer me a job. I want to be able to see clearly. I only want to work here if this is where you want me to work.' And let me tell you, if you do that, you're going to be exactly where God wants you to be in His plan. That's active dependence."

This non-negotiable connects to what I believe to be the main factor behind the extraordinary loyalty of the people who work at Happy State Bank.

> **Pat operates his life and his business on a principle he calls "active dependence." It combines deep trust in God; frequently discussed, right out loud, vigorous and direct action in support of one's goals; and lots and lots of prayer—public, private, each and every day as you work to attain those goals.**

There really is a single, driving reason why so many people stay at Happy State Bank for so long, and it's not what most people think. It's not because of the generosity of the firm in terms of benefits, or the pay, or even the strong sense of personal connection that can arise out of a common commitment to a common cause. All of that helps, but it isn't the main reason people stick around. People stay at Happy State Bank because that's where they feel like they're most successful. Don't misunderstand me; I'm not talking necessarily about people always being promoted. People don't have to feel like they're being promoted all the time in order to feel like they're being successful. We've all met people who work like crazy, spread themselves too thin, and earn lots of promotions, but don't feel like they're being successful. Pat believes that true success lies in what he calls active dependence.

This connects to prayer because it connects to a deep trust in God. It really is a central part of the working culture at Happy State Bank, and it's modeled by Pat and all of his senior people each and every day.

Active dependence is the belief that, with faith in God and hard work on your part, you can become pretty much anything you want to become in life, no matter how unlikely your goal may seem to you at first. And the people who work at Happy State Bank stick around because this workplace allows them to fulfill their own highest aspirations for who they want to be in life. And that's not something you get with just any job.

People expect a great deal from each other here, and they learn to expect a great deal from themselves, too. They set each other up for success, which is the polar opposite of what happens at most organizations.

Active dependence means establishing high standards, taking direct action to fulfill them (that's the "active" part), and then combining prayer with the knowledge that God is always going to open doors for you, your career, and your company (that's the "dependent" part). The "active" and the "dependent" operate simultaneously. Pat believes that all doors are open to him and that God will close one if Pat is not supposed to go through it. For Pat, and for everyone at Happy State Bank, all things are possible until God says otherwise. Every great personal and organizational initiative that connects to this bank has been built on the foundation of active dependence.

> **Active dependence means establishing high standards, taking direct action to fulfill them (that's the "active" part), and then combining prayer with the knowledge that God is always going to open doors for you, your career, and your company (that's the "dependent" part).**

It's not a trick. It's not double-talk. It's not PR. Pat Hickman really has created a corporate working environment in which belief is a fundamental aspect of personal and organizational achievement. This is the belief that your footsteps are guided, that you have an obligation to take action on your own behalf, and that once you start doing what you believe you're supposed to do, the right doors will open for you—whether or not you've got evidence that it's the "logical" next step for you. We read lots of letters from co-owners and former co-owners who thanked Pat for inspiring them to succeed in a career they had once thought impossible. He's trained them to stop thinking that way. People don't wait around for doors to open here.

"I believe that any door I am not supposed to walk through, God will shut," Pat told me one day, "so I just keep doing what I believe I'm supposed to do."

Pat thinks that way. He lives that way. And he's not the only one. He's built a whole company on that principle of active dependence, which is the exact opposite of what most companies train their people to think about career development. And it's worth noting that a whole lot of doors have been held open for him—and for the people who have followed his lead in building and living non-negotiables.

"I would never want anyone to be uncomfortable," Pat says, "but I also want people who work here to know that if they want to pray or if they are with a coworker or customer who wants to pray, then they should go ahead and pray. We don't just permit prayer. We like it."

Pat's wife, Nancy Hickman, told me: "The main thing to understand about Pat is that he just does not make a decision, big or small, without praying first. He prays about his positions and then he walks forward and trusts that if he's going in the wrong direction, God will redirect him and turn him around. A lot of people may not understand that or even believe it, but I watch it at home all the time. He does not take a big step forward unless he's prayed about it first. He also knows that he's got a great group of men and women around him—people he trusts. He really is a very humble man, but what sometimes comes across to people as cockiness is a belief that he can go forward, that God will let him know if He has other plans in mind, and a deep belief in his own people. So, when you work with him or live with him, you just learn to say, 'OK, here we go.' He moves forward, but he's also a lot more humble than most people realize."

NON-NEGOTIABLE #7:
TAKE CARE OF YOUR GOOD EMPLOYEES
AND GET RID OF YOUR BAD ONES

There are a number of non-negotiables on Pat's list that really could improve the performance of every single company on earth if they were adopted by every manager in the organization. I believe this is one of them.

"Take care of your good employees and get rid of your bad ones" is one of those principles that a lot of companies say they observe, but really don't. We've all had experiences, particularly customer service experiences, that proved to us without a doubt that someone was in the wrong job. At Happy State Bank, one of the core operating principles is that proven stars need to get rewards—and proven underperformers need to go. No matter who they are. No matter where they work. No matter how long they've been with the organization.

"I tell people," Pat said during one of our interviews, "that if you want 'just a job,' where you will earn 'just a paycheck,' you need to work somewhere else. We are looking for folks who have a pride and a passion and want a career. And we do right by those people. There are all kinds of rewards waiting for you if you work your way into that group, and all kinds of recognition. We take care of the people who contribute at a high level.

> **At Happy State Bank, one of the core operating principles is that proven stars need to get rewards—and proven underperformers need to go. No matter who they are. No matter where they work. No matter how long they've been with the organization.**

"But guess what? If you're working here, then I also want you to know, right up front, that while we make sure to encourage our best performers, we also identify the worst performers. If you fall into that second category, we give you ideas and instructions on how to improve, and if that doesn't work, we find you an opportunity to flourish elsewhere. Those are the ground rules."

If you contribute consistently, you get rewards. If you underperform consistently, you get coaching, and if you keep on underperforming despite the coaching, you get shown the door.

Every other week, Pat Hickman meets personally with a fresh crop of new employees to make certain the ground rules for this non-negotiable are crystal clear as they begin their time at Happy. But the important thing to understand about Happy State Bank, especially when it comes to this non-negotiable, is *it's not just talk*. It's talk accompanied by action.

"You set out clear expectations," he informed me during one of our interviews, "but that's not all you do. You make sure those expectations take the form of some kind of action. That means you actually have to identify people who aren't performing up to potential, and you actually have to get rid of people. That's where we're different, I guess.

"It's not always a new employee. When you say to yourself 'I'm going to have an absolute on this,' that doesn't mean you single out the new kids. Sometimes, somebody falls off that has been with you a long time. Just a couple of days ago, I had to sit down with a senior, valued member of our team who's in a singular role. There's really no backup and if we were to lose this person, it would probably be mass chaos. And this person is just doing a very poor job in managing his assistant. He's treating her like crap. And that's not how we operate.

"So I was sitting down with my team yesterday, and I said, 'We've got to talk to this guy. He needs to hear the countdown.'"

At Happy State Bank, when the countdown begins, it means you have had "The Talk." It means your job is in jeopardy. Pat told me that the countdown is short. It's one warning, then out.

"And my senior people, including some people who have been with me for a very long time said, 'Pat, we just can't run the risk of losing this guy. If he gets mad and quits, it's going to set us so far behind that we won't be able to catch up. The regulators are going to go crazy. Plus he has A, B, and C skills that we will never, ever be able to replace. We just can't run the risk of losing this person. Pat, please don't start the countdown with this person.'"

As I listened to Pat speak, I thought for a moment about what other CEOs in other companies might say to the senior team in that situation. I had a pretty good idea of what Pat would say though—and I was right.

"And it just made me so damn mad," he went on, "that I know my face turned red.

"I said, 'Look, this one is not up for debate. If his attitude stinks, we can't let that stand. He can't treat our coworkers this way. Period. I don't give a damn if he is the mountaintop for experience in his profession, we are not going to put up with that. I'm starting the countdown. It's an absolute. You don't treat people the way this guy is treating his assistant and get to keep working here.

"Long story short, we had the countdown talk with this person, and he cleaned up his act.

"Big success story, right? But it only happened because we had a clear system in place that says, 'This is what happens when you are really, truly about to lose your job.' And everybody understands that.

"Look: When your kids act up, you've got to tell them, 'Hey son, don't do that.' And if they keep on doing what you said not to do, you've got to do something. If you don't, then you flunk the parenting test. And my kids will tell you, I didn't tell them twice.

"Haven't you ever gone to the doctor's office and you see that kid acting up in the corner? And Mommy is over there going, 'OK, Jimmy, don't do that, Jimmy. I said don't do that. Jimmy I'm going to tell your daddy.'

"And Jimmy keeps doing whatever it is he's doing. Then Mommy says, 'Jimmy, one, two,' and the kid quits. He knows the warning system. She taught him that. She also taught him that nothing mattered until she got to the warning system, and that is ineffective parenting. I feel like if you don't have a warning system and you don't go straight to it, you flunk the parenting test. And it's just the same in a company. If you've got no warning system, and it takes who-knows-how-long to get there, you've got no system. And a manager needs a system.

"So everyone who has the responsibility of managing people here knows that, if you see somebody doing something extraordinary, something has to happen. If the something is extraordinary in a good way, you need to praise the person publicly. And if it's extraordinary in a bad way, the countdown starts. You need to sit down with that person one on one. Praise publicly, reprimand privately. And when you're in that private meeting, you need to get eye to eye with the person and have a very clear discussion—no sugarcoating. You need to say. 'Listen, what you're doing doesn't work. We need you to fix this if you want to stay here.' And if they don't fix it, you've got to fire their butt, no matter who they are.

"And if you don't, you don't ever show the kid that countdown, if you don't ever go one, two, three, and then fire somebody, then you are sacrificing accountability on the team. (And at Happy State Bank the countdown is more like two, one, zero!) I mean if you cave in once, you're a liar. You're dead. You just told everybody that doing X is going to get you fired. How in the world are you going to let someone keep doing X in full view of everyone in the company?

"If your employees see one employee get away with something, and there are no consequences, there is a breakdown. And if they don't get away with something, people notice that, too. People say, 'Look, there is where we can bend the rule over there. But you can't get away there; OK, we all know, don't break that rule because we saw what happened to that employee on that one.' It's really that simple.

"Everyone can make a great first impression. Not everyone can do a great job. When they do, we celebrate them, and we make damn sure everyone knows exactly what they're doing right. When they don't, we work with them to make things better, and if they don't get better, we get rid of them, and we make no apologies for it. Sometimes, people know the story at Happy. They come and say, 'Hey, I want to work here. Look at me smile. See how happy I am?' Then, a week later, you're thinking, *How the hell did that guy con us? Get his little butt out of here.*"

NON-NEGOTIABLE #8:
RESPECT AND APPRECIATE OTHERS!
THERE'S NO DIFFERENCE BETWEEN
OFFICERS AND EMPLOYEES.
WE ARE ALL PEOPLE.

I saw this non-negotiable in action every single time I saw Pat interact with the people who work with him.

Now, I know that sounds like a cliché. I know that if you were to ask 100 CEOs picked at random whether they respect and appreciate their employees, my guess is that you'd get close to 100 "Yes" answers. But I also know that if you asked employees of those same 100 CEOs (anonymously!) whether they felt respected and appreciated by the CEO, you would get a very different answer.

> Happy State Bank employees really do feel like Pat respects them on a personal level—as a peer. What's even more remarkable is how often they volunteer the fact that they want to make him personally proud of their contribution. They want to live up to, or exceed, his expectations.

Believe it or not, though, Happy State Bank employees really do feel like Pat respects them on a personal level—as a peer.

What's even more remarkable is how often they *volunteer* the fact that they want to make him personally proud of their contribution. They want to live up to, or exceed, his expectations.

So maybe you're wondering the same thing I was wondering: *How does he do this? And how does the same basic pattern— mutual respect, the desire to live up to expectations—play out with the employees who report to the leaders of the various departments and branches of the bank?* (Which it does!)

One of the things that Pat is really great at is recognizing people in front of their peers. This habit is deeply woven into the fabric of the bank's working culture, and it's driven by Pat's personal example. I had the opportunity to sit in on a bank officers meeting at Happy State Bank. Pat was there. We were in this big room, and there were 175 bank officers with us. The bulk of the meeting was Pat going around the room and giving each and every one of those 175 people the opportunity to share what they're doing at work, and also the opportunity to share something about what's going on in their lives.

It was so unlike a lot of other officers meeting I've seen CEOs handle. Why? Well, for one thing, the topics were not limited to each person's area of responsibility *within the business,* although that was usually the starting point. Pat also wanted these people to share something important that was happening in their family life, too. It didn't matter whether the individual was a branch manager or in IT or in marketing—whoever they were, Pat wanted to know about what was going in their world, both on a professional level and on a personal level.

So someone might have brought the group up to date on what he was doing in terms of updating an important database for the bank, and also share that the last of his four kids had made the trip off to college this past weekend, and he and his wife had the house to themselves for the first time in 25 years!

What Pat was really doing by facilitating this meeting in this way was *fusing those two worlds of family and business.* He was building a family atmosphere in the workplace, so that each person in the room had a sense of what every other person was experiencing—and supported that person as a fellow human being and a fellow member of the "family." I don't think I've ever seen anything quite like it in the workplace. Pat really cares about *everyone* at the bank.

The truly remarkable thing was that, after each person spoke, Pat was able to make some on-point acknowledgement about exactly where that person was adding value to the bank. He'd say, "I want you all to know that David and his team in IT are doing just a terrific job with this project, and here's why I say that...." And then he would go on to give evidence that showed he was totally up to date on what was working and what the most important contributions in that person's world were. It never felt forced or contrived. And as often as he did that with one person, it didn't take away from the next thing he had to say about the next person who stood up to speak.

I can't tell you how many Happy State Bank employees I interviewed who said things like, "I would never, ever want to let Pat down." That's the kind of respect we are talking about here.

I asked Pat to share his thoughts on how to make sure there really is respect and appreciation in the workplace. Here's what he told me: "What it really comes down to is acknowledging that there's actually no difference between officers and employees.

"We are all people," he went on, "and we are all working toward a common goal. It's like any great championship team: At the end of the season, everyone gets a ring, even the trainers. Yes, there are skill positions, and the people in those positions may be paid more or receive more press, but it takes the whole team to win the game or win the championship. And if any one person starts thinking that the team can't make it without him or her, that person is nuts. Someone who thinks like that makes the whole team suffer.

"So we build respect and appreciation as a team. It's not just how one person operates. It's how the team operates. For instance, we want to make sure that no staff member ever feels uncomfortable in any way as a result of off-color remarks or jokes or anything else. That's an important part of respecting someone else. That kind of disrespect is just not part of our foundation, not a part of the institution we call Happy State Bank. Everyone who works here wants to be appreciated and respected. Everyone has a right to feel that way. And ultimately, it's up to the people within the building—all the directors, all the officers, all the staff—to make sure that happens."

This is not just talk. I can tell you from personal experience *it happens on a personal level* at Happy State Bank, each and every day. Personally, I believe the main reason it happens is that Pat really is comfortable talking to each and every individual in the bank—which is quite rare for the CEO of a bank! It doesn't matter. He values all people, and he treats all people with respect and dignity. That's why everyone feels special in his eyes, and no one wants to let him down.

NON-NEGOTIABLE #9:
STAY QUICK AND NIMBLE, YET
MAKE LONG-TERM DECISIONS

At first, I was a little surprised to find this cumbersome-sounding item among Happy State Bank's non-negotiables. Everything else on the list made such instant intuitive sense, and this one didn't seem to fit at first. Spending some time at the bank branches convinced me, though: Not only is this a critical organizational value, but also it is also a major factor in the bank's success.

Pat explained it to me as follows: "We can react to a customer's request, or respond to an emergency, or take advantage of an expansion opportunity, faster than any other competitor. And the reason for that is that we are quick on our feet. That's an absolute. It's a requirement for working here. We're quick on our feet, and we're going to stay quick on our feet.

> I tell my people never to make a short-term decision that might make us a little money today if they can make a better long-term decision that makes us a lot of money in the long haul. We want our customers to stick around.
>
> —Pat

"So, we make the best decisions we possibly can, we make them pretty rapidly, and we don't second-guess each other. At the same time, though, we also recognize that we are in this for the long haul. Our relationships are what really count. And we know that our profits are only good if they're better than last month or last year. So I tell my people never to make a short-term decision that might make us a little money today if they can make a better long-term decision that makes us a lot of money in the long haul. We want our customers to stick around.

"So you need both halves of that equation: Being quick with a response, and at the same time making a good long-term decision that benefits both the customer and the bank. That is what builds long-lasting relationships.

"Now, in the heat of the battle, sometimes you do have to make a tough decision all by yourself. And when that happens, we want you to know that the bank will stand with you and back you up. That's incredibly important. You're not paid to follow instructions. You are paid to make good judgment calls. And that doesn't just go for managers and loan officers, by the way. That goes for everyone."

A great example of the nimble decision making that makes sense in both the short term and long term came up when I was speaking with Bob Lang, an Amarillo entrepreneur who is a customer of Happy State Bank. Bob's retail operation, a large tire store, was expanding to a second store, and he was looking to get a commercial loan to launch the new store. The problem was that the construction on the store had been significantly delayed. There were all kinds of problems—with the foundation, the phone lines, the city's approval of the driveways, you name it. They were months behind schedule.

One of the loan officers, Scott Martin, reached out to Bob and told him that even though the construction on the store was not at the final stage, he (Scott) wanted to wrap up the paperwork on the commercial loan they had been discussing, and he wanted to do that right away. This was quite an offer, because the collateral for the loan, the physical store itself, was not yet complete!

As Bob Lang recalled, "Scott came to me and said, 'Bobby, I know we're not quite finished yet, but I think I would like to close this out because I don't want this interest rate to change. You have got such a great interest rate on this, and we may never get that rate again. I think we need to lock this in today.' He was taking care of us. So we went ahead and completed the loan even though the store wasn't quite complete."

Usually, of course, the construction has to be done before the loan is finalized. But the story gets even better. After all those months of delays in construction, Bob found out that the city had plans to widen the road in front of the store. "Why they couldn't have done that while we were still under construction, I don't know," Bob recalls, "but there we were, having gotten our loan at that great rate, and I had to call Scott and tell him that we had very little income coming in. And Scott made another great judgment call. Right away, he said, 'Bobby, don't worry about it, we are here for you.' And we got some extra time to pay back the loan. We were able to get back on track once the city finished the roadwork."

Look at what happened here. Most loan officers want to write loans at the highest possible interest rate, but Scott moved quickly to lock in a better rate—and he made a decision that supported the long-term interests of both bank and customer. When he locked in the low rate, he locked in the customer! He also supported the client when the roadwork began—and he locked in that customer's loyalty even more securely.

Two questions: First, how difficult and time-consuming would it have been for a loan officer to make those kinds of decisions on behalf of a client at any other bank? And second, who do you think Bob Lang is going to go to, or recommend, the next time anyone needs financing? Happy State Bank! Good things happen when you empower people.

Notice that Scott had the authority to make this decision. He knew he wouldn't be called on the carpet for it, because he was using the non-negotiable as his guideline!

By the way, Bob Lang also told me: "I would give the people at Happy State Bank the shirt off my back if they asked for it." That's the sound of a satisfied, loyal customer talking!

NON-NEGOTIABLE #10:
SEEK INPUT, SHARE EVERYTHING, HIDE NOTHING, ASK QUESTIONS

Happy State Bank operates very comfortably in a cultural zone that a lot of other companies call "transparency." Here, though, that zone is much larger. People at Happy take transparency to the next level. Anyone in the organization can ask anyone else a question about anything at all, at any time, and expect to receive a polite, accurate answer. They call that "honest, professional adversarialism," a phrase that Pat appeals to often.

Honest, professional adversarialism doesn't mean being unkind or settling a grudge. It just means posing questions that someone else hasn't thought of yet.

Honest, professional adversarialism means putting everything on the table, talking everything over frankly, and, whenever it's appropriate, taking advantage of the expertise of people who might just know more about something than you do. This is a truly great non-negotiable, because it assumes that transparency is really only the starting point. It's part of a larger process of respectful, mutual accountability.

Pat put it this way: "We have a lot of smart people here, and we seek advice from lots of different folks. We believe it's good for lots of different people to ask lots of questions, and we also believe it's important not to take those questions personally. And of course, we don't want you to hide anything. At the same time, we don't want anyone to be mean-spirited when they're asking questions.

> **If I want our people to keep their word and be open about things, then I have to keep my word and be open about things first. And I wouldn't ever want to work for someone who didn't do that.**
>
> **—Pat**

"Honesty and forthrightness always work. It's a great combination. So we make sure we always make time and have time to talk to our coworkers. We don't hide anything from anybody, and we remind each other all the time that we're all the same team, working for the same goals.

"Honest, professional adversarialism doesn't mean being unkind or settling a grudge. It just means posing questions that someone else hasn't thought of yet.

"I know there's a balancing act here, and we work hard to get it right. I always like to remember what the Bible says about communication. It says we should always 'speak the truth in love' (Ephesians 4:15).

"Now, I know I really am responsible for the degree to which people keep their commitments about honesty and forthrightness to each other. Ultimately, that's my job. That means I have to do it first. If I want our people to keep their word and be open about things, then I have to keep my word and be open about things first. And I wouldn't ever want to work for someone who didn't do that.

"I hear stories sometimes about companies where the CEO tells his assistant, 'Now, I want you to go through all the files and delete everything you find in there that's got my signature on it.' What kind of message does that send to the rest of the company when it gets out? And you know that kind of thing does get out. That's not how we do things.

"A while back, the compensation committee on our board of directors went to my chief accountant and said, 'Hey, we've looked at individual pieces of Pat's compensation, but I don't know that we've looked at his total package in a long time. Would you get that to us?

"And the chief accountant came in my office and said, 'Pat, they want to see everything. Do you want to show them everything?' And I said, 'You give them absolutely everything. And by the way, if they ask, my underwear size is size 38, you can give them that, too.' The board of directors is my boss. They have a right to see that.

"And that's the kind of relationship you've got to have. You can't have people on either side of the relationship covering up things. That's certainly not the kind of relationship I expect from the people who report to me. I've told people: 'Hey, if you ever even think there's a hint of unethical, immoral, or illegal behavior going on in my office, and you don't tell me about it, I'll fire your little butt so fast it will turn your head around. And if you're feeling nervous about that responsibility, then you have my permission to go get a couple of tough guys to go with you to hold me accountable. Because I am going to keep my word to you.'"

Another benefit of honest, professional adversarialism is that if you have what you think is a good idea, you can keep plugging for it. My favorite example of this involves the name of the bank, which has emerged as a major branding triumph in the region and the industry as a whole.

A lot of people think the name "Happy State Bank" was Pat's idea, but he will be the first to tell you that he was dead set against it, even though the first bank in the chain really was located in Happy, Texas. The original name of the bank was the First State Bank of Happy, Texas. A problem arose when an opportunity to expand into Stratford, Texas presented itself. There was already a First State Bank in the market. For legal reasons, Pat's bank had to come up with another name. The question was, which one?

An internal team came up with the name "Happy State Bank," and kept pushing for it, even though Pat's initial response was negative. Because the culture celebrated sharing everything, even with the president of the bank, people kept pushing. Didn't the name "Happy State Bank" sum up the emotions, the culture, the *experience* of banking at this bank? Wasn't the name a competitive advantage in a marketplace crowded with *grumpy* banks?

At another bank, the idea would have been dead as the proverbial doornail, if for no other reason than that the man at the top refused to sign off on it. ("I hated the name *Happy State Bank*," Pat told me, "absolutely hated it.") But when a consultant came back with the same recommendation—even after having been warned that Pat didn't want to see the name "Happy State Bank" as a candidate ever again—Pat re-examined his position. The rest is history. The name of the bank is unforgettable—and it's also a powerful brand promise that has dominated everywhere the bank operates.

This story proves to me that honest, professional adversarialism works—and that Pat really does live by it. Honest, professional adversarialism means pushing for the very best answer and not taking things personally when it finally emerges, whatever it may be. It means stepping back, doing your best every single time, based on your own experience and your own instincts, and then finding the best outcome for everyone. And, as the name of the bank proves, honest, professional adversarialism means acknowledging, without hard feelings, when someone else is right—even if you do happen to be the CEO of the bank.

By the way, one of the very best parts of being a Happy State Bank customer is getting that debit card that has the cool Happy State Bank logo on it. Whenever you shop out of the bank's regional market, everyone who sees the card will smile and chuckle, and lots of people will ask, "Is that a real bank?" In and around the Texas Panhandle, though, everyone knows the Happy State Bank experience is for real! You can go to www.HappyBank.com and check it out.

NON-NEGOTIABLE #11: TALK TO EACH OTHER

A lot of people come across this non-negotiable and think, "Well, this one's pretty easy. I already do talk to my people, and they talk to me."

Are you sure?

Very often, we *think* we're talking to people, when actually we're texting them. Or emailing them. Or leaving them voice mail messages.

What we're looking at now is real-time, two-way communication you can see and hear. When Pat Hickman emphasizes "Talk to each other" as an absolute, imperative non-negotiable, here's what he really means: *Get face to face.*

Do that first. If it's at all possible, you want to physically occupy the same space with the people you work with and communicate with. That's the best way to interact about what you're doing together and what your mutual expectations are. That's how you build personal relationships.

The next best replacement for that (if it's absolutely unavoidable) is a phone call or a video call.

Way down on the list of possible options—far, far below having a personal, face-to-face discussion or a personal voice-to-voice discussion—is leaving a voice mail, sending a text, or sending an email. Those things don't support a personal relationship in the same way a real-time conversation does. So they shouldn't be the main way you interact with the people you count on and who count on you.

> **People are more likely to be polite to each other and respect each other if they are looking each other in the eye. It's harder to be rude to a colleague. It's harder to say "No." It's harder to be tacky when the person is standing right in front of you.**

So think about this non-negotiable for a moment. Here is how Happy State Bank demands that its people communicate:

- Ideally: face to face
- Or, if that's impossible: voice to voice
- And then, way down on the list: via text, email, or voice mail

And here is how most companies today operate—the exact opposite:

- Ideally: text, email, or voice mail
- Or sometimes: voice to voice
- And then, maybe occasionally: face to face

This is one of those non-negotiables that a lot of business leaders tend to push back on. They talk a lot about the mobile workplace and about how technology liberates them and how different generations interpret things like email messages and text messages. I'm not arguing any of that. All I'm saying is that accountability is all about a personal relationship, and that people tend to have stronger personal relationships when they can see and hear each other. So at the very least, you might want to consider relying more heavily on voice-to-voice communication and video-conferencing than on email messages and text messages, because email messages and text messages are *inherently imper-sonal.* If you rely on them to run your business, you will find that accountability is weak. Why? Because the relationships are weak.

Some companies today are eliminating or greatly reducing working from home. They feel that there is a loss of "team" and communication suffers. Being able to actually speak with some-one face to face is the best way to communicate.

Here's how Pat put it to me: "If people would just talk to each other, in person, life would be a whole lot easier. Talk in person first. Your backup is to talk by phone. I tell our people, 'Please, please, please use email as a last resort.' You want to know why? Because people are more likely to be polite to each other and respect each other if they are looking each other in the eye. It's harder to be rude to a colleague. It's harder to say 'No.' It's harder to be tacky when the person is standing right in front of you."

Happy State Bank is an in-person kind of operation. That may sound "so last century" to some people in the banking industry—or any other industry—but I can tell you that the employees and the customers prefer it that way, and their opin-ion counts for something.

My favorite example of the "Talk to Each Other" non-nego-tiable in action is a little ritual Pat calls MBBD.

That stands for *Management by Beer Drinking.*

Once a week, more or less, he and his top people sit down after hours and discuss strategy over a six-pack. Or two. The beer is always paid for out of private funds, not bank funds, and if you don't want to drink a beer, you can drink something non-alcoholic.

The point is not to get drunk, of course, but to relax, enjoy each other's company, and brainstorm about the week to come. It's a time to be with each other. Somehow, it wouldn't work quite as well if everyone just texted in ideas while they were drinking beer at home. Pat told me, "Some of our best ideas have come out of those conversations where we were all sitting around together, relaxed and enjoying each other's company."

Like a lot of Pat's non-negotiables, this one isn't for everyone, and it may take some getting used to if you're used to something else. But if you decide to adopt this non-negotiable for yourself and/or your team, you will quickly learn something very cool about this way of doing business. People buy into it, and as a result, it works.

NON-NEGOTIABLE #12:
SOMETIMES WE MAKE A MISTAKE.
ADMIT IT AND FIX IT FAST.

This non-negotiable applies to interactions with colleagues *and* interactions with customers. If you try to apply it just to one group or the other, it doesn't work for either group.

At Happy State Bank, the attitude is: *Mistakes happen. Get over it.* Everyone makes mistakes. Unless you make the same mistake over and over and over, you find out that mistakes are quickly forgiven. What Pat—and everyone else—is picky about is making the situation worse. How do you do that? By saying that no mistake was made, or making excuses for it, or not trying to fix it. That just compounds the mistake.

In *No More Excuses,* I discuss how this weakens us as people—whether we're making them or accepting them (page 24). It limits us and our future. Successful people do not make excuses. They take responsibility for mistakes and fix them. That's what Pat instructs his team to do.

Pat told me: "The beautiful thing about really meaning it when you say you want to move on from mistakes is that people eventually start to relax. They realize that you mean it when you tell them you want them to do their very best, even if that means making a mistake now and then. They realize you're not out to play gotcha with them. So people relax, people accept that mistakes are part of the deal, and everyone can focus on what has to happen next. And they do want to get it right. I never met anyone who wanted, deep down, to do a terrible job. **You've got**

to do what's right for the relationship. You've got to fix the problem, whatever it is.

"Once you make it clear that you're out to remove all the obstacles that stand in the way of someone fixing a mistake, my experience is that they usually want to fix the problem. Every once in a while, you run into an exception to that, but by and large, you find that once people can relax on the job, they really do want to fix the mistake.

"It really helps to say 'I'm sorry.' The faster you tell a customer or coworker that you were sincerely sorry for a problem, the better off everyone will be, and the longer that customer or coworker will stick around.

"Someone told me that back in the days when prisoners had to wear a ball and chain, there was a very strange thing that happened. Every night when they went to bed, each of the prisoners had to pick that ball up and set it in the bed with them. And the first thing they would do in the morning was to reach down and get that ball and set it down on the ground. Eventually, though, they'd complete their sentence, and after they got their freedom, they would make it back home and sleep in their own bed. Then, when they'd wake up in the morning, the first thing they would do is reach down for an iron ball that wasn't there. They'd done their time, they'd been unshackled, but they'd been shackled for so long that they'd forgotten that they didn't have that ball to drag around anymore. Sometimes, that happens when people get used to not fixing the mistake, not saying 'I'm sorry.'

"We bought some branches from a big multinational bank, but I won't tell you the name. Let's call them BigBank. We brought these people over to a new way of doing business, a new standard of saying 'I'm sorry.' They were so shackled with rules, with regulations, with company crap, that they weren't allowed to do what needed to be done to take care of the customer. We gave them freedom. We took away the iron ball. If they could learn not to reach for the iron ball every morning, we held on to them. Most of them figured out before too long that they didn't have anything heavy strapped on to their ankle anymore.

"I'll give you an example of how well that transition worked. We have a little thing called a $10 Texas Scratch Pad. This is a little pad that has ten sequentially numbered $1 bills in it. People buy them for Christmas, they use them for stocking stuffers, for anniversaries, graduations, and stuff like that. And we give our tellers ten of them each, and we say, 'Use these to fix the mistake. Use them to calm down customers who are upset about something. By the way, if you run out of these, come get some more. It's totally unaudited. We trust you.'"

> **I never met anyone who wanted, deep down, to do a terrible job.**

Let me pause for just a moment to clarify what Pat is saying here about the scratch pads. *The bank doesn't keep track of who takes these bills or why.* So if you give a scratch pad to your cousin, or if you put them in your purse, management will never know. That's the message: We trust you. Not exactly the message you get from BigBank!

Back to Pat: "We told our former BigBank people, along with everyone else: 'We're not going to ask you who you gave these scratch pads to. We just want you to use them whenever there is a mess-up. If there is a mistake, or a customer is unhappy for some reason, this is one of the tools in your arsenal.

"So whenever a customer comes in and they're unhappy, first off, we want you to listen to them. Second, tell them, 'We're going to help.' Then we want you to hand them a Texas Scratch Pad. And if they're still mad, hand them another one, quick.

"We want you to do whatever you've got to do to make those people happy. You let them know you care and you let them know that you're here to get them over whatever bump they've encountered in the road. It works!

"Well, I happened to be in one of the branches one day right after we bought the BigBank branches. And this lady comes in and she's hopping mad. And I'm visiting with another customer, but I hear the conversation going on in the background with the teller. And she's talking to her teller and she says, 'I banked with you for eight years, but this is the third time your bank is sold. Every time it was sold, the service got worse, and people just tried to sell me things I didn't need. I'm not going to go through it again. I'm going to change banks.'

"And the teller she was talking to had already made the transition. She had already gotten rid of that iron ball. She wanted to fix the problem. I knew, because she said, 'Please give us another chance. You're going to really like this new bank. We are here to take care of you. You know what, here's a $10 Texas Scratch Pad—just to thank you for coming in today.'

"And you know what? She wasn't done. The teller said, 'Guess what? Our CEO is over here. Just come over here and talk to him and let him tell you what kind of bank you're with now. Please!'

"So she brings this lady over to me and as she's sitting there, the customer tells me the story all over again about how she's so upset. She loves her teller, she doesn't want to leave her teller, but this is the third time her bank has changed names in the last five years. She was done with us.

"And I said, 'Well, did we give you a $10 Texas Scratch Pad?'

"She said, 'Yeah, and that kind of makes me feel bad. I told her I don't want it. I thought she might get in trouble.'

"I said to the teller, 'So give her another one.' And the teller did.

"The customer said, 'No, it's OK, I don't want that.'

"And I said, 'You know what, I think she'd really like a T-shirt. Let's give her a Happy State Bank T-shirt. That would probably close the deal.'

"And she laughed and said, 'I don't need a T-shirt.'

"Then the teller said, 'Hey, I've got a baseball cap.' She went and got it. It was a pink baseball cap with our logo on it. And then all of a sudden the customer said, 'Well, I do love pink.' And she smiled and she took the cap from the teller.

"I said, 'We just got you. Am I right? We just got you and we kept you, didn't we?'

"She said, 'Yes.'

"And she did stay. She's one of our best customers. She loves us! We tell all our employees to do that kind of thing.

"Now, we also made a point of telling the people from Big-Bank, 'Listen, we know most of you have been community bankers before BigBank bought your bank. Maybe you remember what it was like to be unshackled. When BigBank bought you, what happened? You got shackled. Well, we want to give you that freedom again.'

"Now, don't get me wrong—we paid attention to what the former BigBank people were doing with our customers. Some of them needed coaching, and some weren't right for our bank. We were a little concerned about the big bank habits that they might have picked up. We've had issues before in hiring people who have never worked at community banks, and we've ended up firing some of them, or some of them just quit after a very short period of time. They just couldn't handle making decisions. The lack of structure killed them. They were still reaching for that iron ball. They couldn't get used to being unshackled, and we had to let them go.

"But most people from the big banks made the transition very well—like that teller did. She knew there was no rule about how many scratch pads you could give a customer. She wanted to make it right, and she did.

"We told all the former BigBank people, 'Guess what? New rule. You've got to think now. You've got to do what's right for the relationship. You've got to fix the problem, whatever it is.'

"If someone before us had a problem listening to this customer, we've got to acknowledge that mistake, quick, and we've got to fix it. That's the way we do business."

NON-NEGOTIABLE #13: GIVE BACK—GET INVOLVED IN YOUR COMMUNITY. THIS IS CONSIDERED PART OF YOUR JOB AT THIS BANK.

Pat told me: "If you work at this bank, it's considered part of your job to get involved with your community. We meet lots of new people and have lots of banking opportunities when we are out and about. Being part of your community makes you more valuable to the bank, and that usually results in your paycheck looking better, too. Plus, it just plain feels good when you get involved in projects that provide for greater good. So get out there and do it!"

If you didn't know this was Happy State Bank, you might think that only management-level people get out and get involved in the community. But because you *do* know what bank we're talking about, you're probably not surprised to learn that tellers, administrative people, and everybody else at Happy is expected to get involved in the local organizations they're passionate about. About 95 percent of the team gets out to participate in the community.

Ben Franklin used to advocate "doing well by doing good." That's exactly what Pat is talking about here—both at the individual level and as an organization, Pat's entire operation is totally committed to making a positive difference in each and every one of the communities where Happy State Bank does business.

Why? First and foremost, because it's the right thing to do. And second, because it's one of the most effective means of marketing out there! Those two interests do not have to compete with one another. In fact, in Pat's world, they operate on exactly the same track.

For instance: Pat loves buying scoreboards for local high school or college teams that need them. That's a very easy decision. You help the local team, and you get the bank's name out there prominently in front of everyone in the community. That's a win-win, no matter what the score of the actual game is.

Pat's entire operation is totally committed to making a positive difference in each and every one of the communities where Happy State Bank does business. About 95 percent of the team gets out to participate in the community.

Here's another example. More than a decade ago, Happy State Bank opened up a kid-friendly "bank" at Sleepy Hollow Elementary School in Amarillo. The program teaches kids about real-world issues like savings, interest, and money management—and helps teachers complete an important part of the curriculum. Kids run the "bank," and kids make real deposits into real accounts. Again, the community involvement serves a dual purpose: It provides an important service, teaching financial literacy to young people, and helping teachers. At the same time, it raises the bank's profile among teachers and the families of the students. Today, Happy State Bank runs a "Banks in Schools" program like that in 27 schools, for well over 1,000 kids! Subsequent to this program being run for a while, the U.S. Treasury Department sought out Happy State Bank and one other bank to conduct research about children's banking habits after they became adults. That was a great honor.

That's just one of remarkable ways the bank and its people give back to the community. There are dozens of community programs like that—probably hundreds if you count all the ways that Happy State Bank employees opt to give back on their own.

Renee McNeely told me: "Officers here do a lot of things in the community. Sometimes when I get preoccupied with other things, I realize how much I miss that, and I make a point of getting back into the rhythm of working with my colleagues on the community programs. So we have something coming up soon where we feed all of the Canyon Independent School District teachers. I love that one. They cook hamburgers and we serve them. I find that fulfilling. You're side by side with your fellow officers doing something for someone else. You're so proud because you put on your Happy State Bank shirt and everyone says, 'Hey, the Happy People are here.' And that's what we are. There's a connection you have with people when you know you're getting involved to give, not to take."

NON-NEGOTIABLE #14:
PRODUCE, DAMN IT!

This is important. It so important that it even has its own acronym: PDI!

Everyone at Happy State Bank understands that privileges only come when you produce, when you perform. Customers rely on it and the co-owners around you rely on it as well.

We make no apologies about why we are here. We are here to produce. We expect excellence from ourselves and from each other. We expect lots of quality and lots of quantity. We expect them both at the same time. We expect people to do it all. We believe that everyone who works here is a superstar. There is no room for mediocrity or going through the motions. It takes everyone doing an exceptional job to make this place run right, run profitably, every single day.

—PAT

Pat told me: "If you work here, you figure out pretty quickly that you're going to have a problem if you show up for work but you miss your family reunion. You know what else, though? You're also going to figure something else out. You're going to have just as big a problem if you take the day off to go to your family reunion but you don't arrange for someone else to cover for you while you're gone. Not only that, you're going to have a problem if you come back from your family reunion, or any other event, and you don't make up all the work you were supposed to do while you were gone.

"You'll see a lot of employee cars in our parking lots on weekends and evenings. That's PDI! I talk to people a lot about how *family first* and PDI! work together. One of the things that I say to our people is, 'Don't you ever gripe about somebody taking time off for a family event, because the next time it's going to be you. And it may not be a family event. It maybe be something else, but whatever it is, you are there to help pick up the slack when she's gone, because she's going to be there to pick up the slack when you're gone.'

"We make no apologies about why we are here. We are here to produce. We expect excellence from ourselves and from each other. We expect lots of quality *and* lots of quantity. We expect them both at the same time. We expect people to do it all.

"We believe that everyone who works here is a superstar. There is no room for mediocrity or going through the motions. It takes *everyone* doing an exceptional job to make this place run right, run profitably, every single day. This place gives a lot, and it expects a lot, too. So *produce, damn it!*"

NON-NEGOTIABLE #15: LAUGH AT WORK.

Yes—this really is a non-negotiable. You might think that it's impossible to mandate a policy of people finding things to laugh about at work. But Happy State Bank proves that it isn't. As usual, Pat Hickman leads the way through the strength of his personal example.

Pat told me: "I was born handsome, instead of rich, so that means I have to work for a living. I figure, if I've got to work somewhere, at least I want to enjoy where I'm working. That's why I made it a rule that you had to be a happy person in order to work here. And part of being a happy person means you have to be able to laugh at yourselves and others without hurting anyone's feelings.

"I figure if we have to work, then dang it, let's have some fun!

"Let's tell jokes. Let's send each other funny emails. Let's make fun of each other. All with respect, of course. We never want to make anyone feel uncomfortable. But dang it, *I* feel uncomfortable when people act like there's nothing that could possibly be funny when you work for a bank. Wrong!

You might think that it's impossible to mandate a policy of people finding things to laugh about at work. But Happy State Bank proves that it isn't.

"So yes, let's laugh. The louder, the better. That means laughter is officially encouraged by management around here. We don't want any sourpusses loitering around the place for too long. And yes, dammit, you will be fired if you don't find a reason to laugh—at least once in a while!" (He says all this with a smile, of course. But he means it.)

Pat's own bizarre sense of humor—most of it self-deprecating, all of it empowering—drives this non-negotiable. I'll give you just one example. Most companies have sick days and personal days. Happy State Bank has those, too, but they also have another kind of day off that Pat invented: *The Crappy Day*. It's nowhere in the handbook, but everyone knows that they are entitled to one Crappy Day each year.

The idea here is that we all have a crappy day once in a while. There's nothing wrong with that. Just don't bring it in to work! Call in and let your colleagues know you're taking a crappy day.

172

Sometimes, Pat will spot someone who's got a bit of an attitude problem that day. It happens to the best of us. He'll walk up to that person and he'll ask: "Hey, did you take your crappy day? No? Well, do you need to?"

From time to time some people do just that, take a Crappy Day, but after digging deeper, I discovered that most of the co-owners at Happy State Bank never need to take a crappy day. Only about four or five people actually take one per year. They're happy!

NON-NEGOTIABLE #16:
EVERY JOB IS YOUR JOB. THERE'S NO SUCH THING AS "NOT MY JOB."

In support of this non-negotiable, Pat says simply: "Don't be haughty or pretentious. There is no such thing as a job that is beneath your doing it. Show that servant's heart."

"Every job is your job" is certainly an admirable standard. But is it really a non-negotiable, as we've defined it in this book? Is it something every single person at Happy State Bank practices, every single day? If you're like me, when you hear this one for the first time, you're probably a little bit skeptical that any company could actually meet that standard consistently.

I know why you feel that way. It's the same reason I did. It doesn't match up with your experience.

> **If a random customer can call that company up, reach a human being with ease, explain his or her problem to that human being, and get the problem resolved by that same human being, without having to explain the problem again to someone else, then the company really does have a culture where job titles don't matter.**

I've been writing, speaking, and helping organizations grow since 1993. Over the years, I've worked with people from thousands of different companies. I've run my own business. I will go out on a limb and say that I've done an above-average job of keeping up with the different customer-first movements in American business, and I've been a customer, just like you, and here's the point. I've heard all kinds of companies say something that sounded vaguely like what you just heard from Pat, some variation on: "We are all here to get the same job done, and no job title is ever going to get in the way of that."

You read something like that, or see it on a commercial. Then what happens?

You call the company up about some problem you're having. You do your best to navigate the "push 1 for this push 2 for that" obstacle course that is built in to the phone system. Eventually, you reach a human being. The human being says, "How can I help you?"

Already, you can tell that's a trick question. But you go ahead and explain your problem anyway. And then what do you hear? Something like this:

"That's not my department. Hold on."

Am I right? You know I am.

Then you get transferred. Then a new person asks that same trick question: "How can I help you?" And of course, you get to explain your problem all over again, from scratch, which makes your mood so much more appealing for everyone involved. If you're lucky, you actually get a hearing from a human being about what it is you're calling about.

If you're not, someone else says "That's not my job," or the equivalent, and you get transferred to a third person. (That happens more than most companies care to admit.) By the time you reach that third person, you are steamed. And you don't really want to hear anything about how everyone is doing the same job and job titles and departments don't matter.

Companies talk like that a lot. The problem is that most companies don't back up their words with actions.

So if you're like me, you hear a bank talk to its employees about how "Every job is your job," and you think—*BS*.

Well, guess what. When you call Happy State Bank, not only do you avoid the whole "push 1 for this, push 2 for that" nonsense (go ahead, call them and check), but the person who answers the phone is personally responsible for solving your problem in such a way that you only have to explain it once.

You read right. That individual who picked up the phone may have to go elsewhere to figure out what the answer to your problem is, or may have to call you back with the best solution rather than solve it for you then and there, but he or she *will* be your point of contact until the issue is resolved. That's the way they do business at Happy State Bank, and it's as a direct result of this non-negotiable.

The words "That's not my department" and "You'll have to call back when Jim's here" and "Let me transfer you to someone who can help you" have all been officially removed from the acceptable vocabulary during interactions with customers. And so have all the subtle variations on those words. The person you explained the problem to has the job of working through it with you until you are happy, regardless of his or her job title. And that's a direct result of this non-negotiable. Happy State Bank wants happy customers!

Now Pat will tell you that getting transferred once in a while will happen, and every now and then someone does say something stupid like, "Joe isn't here right now and he's the only one who knows the answer"—and that drives him crazy—but 19 times out of 20, they get it right on the first call.

This presents us with a good litmus test. Any company that *says* its entire workforce is all about serving the customer, regardless of job title, now has a clear standard to hit. If a random customer can call that company up, reach a human being with ease, explain his or her problem to that human being, and get the problem resolved by that same human being without having to explain the problem again to someone else, then the company really does have a culture where job titles don't matter. If they don't pass the Happy State Bank test, then the company and all its customers are still prisoners of the "not my job" syndrome.

NON-NEGOTIABLE #17:
DON'T WATCH THE CLOCK—THE BANK DOESN'T, AND YOU SHOULDN'T EITHER

"Don't take advantage of this bank," Pat tells his people, "because it will never take advantage of you."

Happy State Bank is great at giving people lots of time off, whether it's for family fun or sickness, or even the occasional bad day. If you need time, you take the time you need. But it's a part of the agreement that there are also times when the bank needs people to burn some midnight oil to get the job done and meet deadlines. They call that "harvest time." When you're on a farm and it's time to harvest the crop, you harvest the crop. That's just how it is. Translation: This is no place for "eight to fivers."

"The bank respects your time, so you need to respect the bank's time. I'm very serious about that. If you steal time from this company, it's the same as walking over to the vault and stealing money. Don't steal time. We are more than happy to give you that time off for family. That's what counts—family time. But we damn well expect you get your work done. Now, it may be that you need to work a little bit later one night to meet all of your commitments. If that's what you need to do, that's what you need to do! But if you leave us hanging in the lurch, there is going to be a serious heart-to-heart when you get back. That's just as important an absolute as *family first*."

Those two values complement each other—they don't compete with each other as they do at a lot of companies. Co-owner Cari Roach, whom I've mentioned earlier, pointed out that at other banks where she had worked, you *had* to watch the clock in order to move up the career ladder. "If you didn't put in the hours, you weren't considered for promotion," Cari recalled.

"The management said all kinds of things about being family-friendly, but their actions said otherwise. You had to put your family second if you wanted to get promoted. And putting in those hours didn't necessarily mean doing more work. It just meant you put in the hours. Here, it's very different. People take the time they need, and they make sure they get their jobs done. When the bank needs them during 'harvest time,' they're there."

> Happy State Bank is great at giving people lots of time off. But it's a part of the agreement that there are also times when the bank needs people to burn some midnight oil to get the job done and meet deadlines. They call that "harvest time." When you're on a farm and it's time to harvest the crop, you harvest the crop. That's just how it is. Translation: This is no place for "eight to fivers."

If you are sitting around waiting for 5 o'clock to roll around, you won't last very long at Happy State Bank. By the same token, a few people spend too much time at the bank. Pat makes sure management intervenes there, too. He insists on the importance of finding the right balance between work and family.

NON-NEGOTIABLE #18:
DON'T EVER FORGET THAT IT'S OTHER PEOPLE'S MONEY

I think the entire financial crisis of 2008-2009 could have been avoided if everyone in Pat's industry had adopted this non-negotiable.

Remember the graphics I showed you a little earlier in the book that illustrated the difference between how Happy State Bank performed and how everyone else in the industry performed during the Great Recession? Here is the graph again if you need another look:

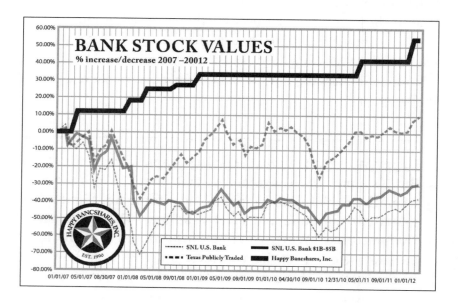

Plenty of people have asked me *why* Happy State Bank came through the financial crisis of 2008-2009 with such great numbers, when so many other banks struggled. In a way, this whole book is the big answer to that question. But there's a more narrowly focused answer, too, and it lies inside this non-negotiable.

At Happy State Bank, each and every co-owner is obliged to remember that the money belongs to someone else. Each co-owner knows that he or she has a personal moral responsibility to act in good faith as a representative of the depositors of the bank and the investors of the bank too—not just in words, but in deeds—not just in the short term, but in the long term—not just once in a while, but all the time.

Some banks didn't do well by that responsibility in the period leading up to the Great Recession.

They *said* all the right things about being responsible trustees for the funds people asked them to take care of, but their actions didn't back their words. They often played for short-term wins that made long-term success for their depositors less likely or even impossible. They often played the game like the rules only mattered some of the time. In short, they acted like it was their money. That's not how Happy State Bank does business.

This non-negotiable translates to a pretty simple principle: Happy State Bank is dead serious when it comes to taking care of the dollars with which it has been entrusted.

> **On any given month, with more than 12,000 notes in the bank, they have less than 20 loans total that are 30 days past due. Likewise, they have more than $1.5 billion loaned out and less than $1 million is ever 30 days past due. They are serious about protecting the assets of their depositors and their investors.**

Pat told me: "We are entrusted by our customers with their money, and we never, ever forget that it's their money, not ours. We are entrusted by our stockholders with their investment dollars, too. We never forget that's their money, either. That means we have to make damn sure that the money we loan out is loaned responsibly, and also that it is paid back in a timely manner. So if someone just plain doesn't have the collateral to justify a certain loan, then we don't make that loan.

"Then there's the other side of the process. Every now and then, after we make a loan, we have to work with our customers to help them live up to their end of the deal, which means we have to collect past dues and fees. Also any overdrafts. That's our job. In each case, we're giving people the opportunity to do the right thing. We are serious about our work, and we believe it is righteous work that we do. We keep our commitments to our depositors and our investors."

Texas is one of, if not the most, productive agriculture states in the nation, and Happy State Bank is (according to the FDIC) the second largest ag-lending bank in the state of Texas. They understand "harvest time."

On any given month, with more than 12,000 notes in the bank, they have less than 20 loans total that are 30 days past due. Anyone can go on the FDIC website, look this up, and verify it. Likewise, they have more than $1.5 billion loaned out and less than $1 million is ever 30 days past due. (This also can be verified on the FDIC website.) They are serious about protecting the assets of their depositors and their investors.

Pat told me that during the period leading up to the great recession, there were plenty of people who would fill out forms falsely and apply for loans they couldn't afford. In keeping with this non-negotiable, the loan officer would have to ask, "Do you really make $150,000 year?" And the applicant would say "Naw, I make $90,000 a year."

Then the loan officer would ask, "So why does it say $150,000 on your application?" And the answer would come back that the person representing Such-and-Such Mortgage Company had told him that's what he had to have on the application in order to qualify for the loan.

There were a whole lot of "inflated" loan applications like that, not just in Texas but all over the country, in the years leading up to the big economic collapse. A lot of banks just went along for the ride and approved the loans. Happy State Bank turned down those applications. Its investors and depositors were—and are—quite happy about that!

NON-NEGOTIABLE #19:
BE AN OWNER, NOT A MANAGER

As I mentioned earlier, each and every "employee" of Happy State Bank really is an owner. That's because stock in the bank is part of the compensation package. Everyone who works there is known as a "co-owner" rather than an "employee"—because that's what everyone really is! The employee stock ownership plan (ESOP) is the largest single stockholder and has close to 10 percent of the company stock. This says a lot about how much they love their employees and how much the employees love the bank.

You might think this particular non-negotiable irrelevant to every organization that doesn't make its employees literal, fiscal co-owners of the enterprise. I'll take issue with that. I will share my reasons with you in a moment. Right now, though I want you to listen to what Pat had to say when I asked him to explain the *difference* between an owner and a manager.

"There is a vast difference between the two." Pat told me. "Owners have to take all the factors into consideration when they make a decision, not just what is the least costly thing to do or the easiest thing to do at the moment. Owners have to think about what makes sense for the whole bank in the long term, not just what makes sense for one person, or a small group of people, in the short term. Managers usually make selfish decisions. Owners can't afford to do that.

"So I am always reminding people that, in order to work here, you really do have to be willing to think like an entrepreneur. Of course, if you've never thought that way before, we know it takes a little practice. And that's OK. But eventually, you do have to take off the 'manager' hat and put on the 'owner' hat. It means we respect you enough to manage your own time. It means you need to be constantly looking for new opportunities to cut costs and increase revenues. It means we want to hear from you about new ideas you come up with for making this bank a better, happier place to work. At the end of the day, we know we have to treat you like what we want you to be.

"That's why we treat you like a co-owner of a competitive business in a very competitive industry—because that's what we are, and that's the level where we need you to contribute. So we treat you with respect. We don't treat you like an employee and we don't treat you like a manager. We treat you like this is what you have chosen to do with your life.

"I mean, this bank is my vocation. It's not a hobby for me. It's what I do. And that's how we want everyone to look at what they do all day here—as a vocation, not as a hobby.

"I always ask the folks in Happy Beginnings, when we talk about this absolute—do you treat a rental car differently than your own, or do you treat an apartment rental differently than a home you own? Of course, they all agree that they do."

> Treating people "like they own the place" requires a lot more than just giving them a stock option. It requires showing them respect and creating an environment where their contributions are truly valued. That's just as important as how you compensate them financially— probably more important.

Now, if you happen to be a business leader or the owner of a company, I have a challenge for you. Before you dismiss this non-negotiable as irrelevant to your organization, let me ask you this: If you treat people like owners, aren't they more likely to *perform* like owners?

Leave aside for now the question of how you compensate your people financially. How do you compensate them *emotionally* for choosing to invest their careers with your company? Do you treat them with respect? Do you make it easy for them to see their contributions as a vocation, as their life's calling? Do you call them something other than employees? Do they *act* like something other than employees? Do they show up early and stay late when circumstances warrant, without you having to talk them into it?

Probably the biggest mistakes I've made in business were people mistakes. I undervalued the people on my team and then wondered why they didn't take the success of our organization as seriously as I did. I assumed it was because I was the owner and I actually made an excuse for their actions by saying, "Owners just work harder. They care more." What I should have been doing was figuring out how to change how I was treating them so that everyone felt like owners, so everyone felt that they were in a place where their presence was appreciated, and so that everyone felt they were serving their personal mission as well.

Treating people "like they own the place" requires a lot more than just giving them a stock option. It requires showing them respect and creating an environment where their contributions are truly valued. That's just as important as how you compensate them financially—probably more important. And that's what this non-negotiable is really all about.

Pat models this non-negotiable on a personal level for everyone, of course.

The result: Valued, trusted, engaged employees! Let me give you an example of what I mean. One evening, he was leaving the office when he saw his head of IT at his desk— still working.

Pat asked him how things were going, and the IT guy said he and his team were working late to accommodate a switch over in systems. Pat found out that the entire IT team expected to be there until 1:30 in the morning! No one complained, no one talked about how unfair "management" was being. They were all in this together. The job had to get done, and it had to get done that night.

That's being an owner, not a manager!

Pat called his wife, Nancy, to double-check on the family schedule and to let her know he was coming home to change and then return to the office. Pat picked up another executive, grabbed some pizza, and returned to the office to support the IT department.

That's being an owner, not a manager, too!

It goes both ways. Always. Which is why everyone around Pat is committed to busting their collective butt to achieve the vision that he lays out for Happy State Bank.

NON-NEGOTIABLE #20:
"TRUST IN THE LORD WITH ALL YOUR HEART, AND LEAN NOT ON YOUR OWN UNDERSTANDING; IN ALL YOUR WAYS ACKNOWLEDGE HIM AND HE WILL DIRECT YOUR PATH" (PROVERBS 3:5-6).

The final non-negotiable on Happy State Bank's list has to do with personal faith.

Now, you might imagine that a non-negotiable like this is all about making sure that every one of Happy State Bank's co-owners worships in basically the same way. But you'd be wrong.

This non-negotiable is all about personal courage—the courage to follow a higher calling, the courage to assume that your life has a purpose. As I've shared with you elsewhere in this book, Pat's beliefs are never a secret to anyone. He's more than willing to proclaim his personal faith in Jesus Christ. It is the defining factor of his life, his identity, and his career. Faith is how he conducts business and everything else—and he doesn't mind saying so, right out loud. But he doesn't use this 20th non-negotiable to make sure *you* have a personal relationship with Jesus Christ. (There are plenty of Happy State Bank co-owners who don't.)

Pat uses this final non-negotiable to celebrate the role of a higher purpose in his own life, and to support anyone else who experiences that sense of being guided by a higher purpose—and wants to celebrate it. This last non-negotiable is the ultimate defense of the Happy State Bank culture: The right of each person to celebrate a sense of guiding, higher purpose in life, *as he or she defines that purpose.* It's a very personal issue, of course, but Pat reserves the right to mark it off as being of central importance to his life, and he reserves the right to let others do the same if they so choose.

> This last non-negotiable is the ultimate defense of the Happy State Bank culture: The right of each person to celebrate a sense of guiding, higher purpose in life, as he or she defines that purpose.

One day, Pat said to me, "Good luck only explains so much. This is really where the *dependence* part of *active dependence* comes in. Through relying on the Holy Spirit to guide and direct, we trust Him and depend on Him to direct us."

For anyone who doubts the existence of a higher purpose who guides human undertakings as a whole, and Pat's undertakings in particular, Pat has plenty of respect, and plenty of great stories to tell, too. Those stories are all about God opening doors for him.

My favorite example of this has to be the story I shared a little earlier—how the bank name his team came up with, the name that Pat vetoed and dug in his heels against, kept floating back to his desk like a feather blown by the wind, until he adopted the name and changed the industry with it! Now the name "Happy State Bank" seems not only just like a stroke of branding genius, but also as natural as Pat's own middle name. If you want to say it was mere chance that kept Pat coming back to that particular door, be my guest. I'm inclined to believe it was something bigger and more important.

To what does J. Pat Hickman attribute his success, and the success of Happy State Bank? I've heard Pat answer this question directly: "We're successful because I surround myself with the right people, and because Jesus loves me, and because I pay attention to that. That's who I am. I'd love to sit here and tell you I'm a genius, and I could talk about strategy with you if you want, but the truth is that the Good Lord has directed this bank and I pay attention to that. Everything we have accomplished is based on the fact that we've relied on our Father in Heaven."

One outsider Pat shared that answer with said, "Wow—nobody's ever given me that kind of response before. I appreciate your boldness."

Pat said: "I'm afraid not to."

That kind of higher purpose goes by any number of different names in any number of different traditions. Pat describes it as a personal relationship with Jesus Christ. I describe it as my personal relationship with the Creator. How do you want to describe it? If the answer is important to you, and maybe it is, this final non-negotiable is here for you.

THE ENDURING POWER OF NON-NEGOTIABLES

I can't tell you exactly how many Happy State Bank co-owners, customers, and stakeholders I ran into who told me, in one way or another, that they would do just about anything to avoid letting down Pat Hickman. I can tell you that there were hundreds of such people, each with a story of his or her own about the enduring power of Pat's non-negotiables as they had impacted his or her life. And I can tell you that if I included all of those stories here, this book would be about the size of a telephone directory.

I have tried to incorporate some of those stories. To close this section of the book, I want to share one remarkable document. It demonstrates the extraordinary *personal and organizational power to achieve full potential waiting to be leveraged from a consciously designed non-negotiable way of life. Here it is:*

Pat,

As you may know, I am expecting my baby any day now, and I will not be coming back to work once she is born. I wanted to take the opportunity while I am still here to tell you what working for Happy has meant to me…. You gave me, a very young and inexperienced girl, opportunities that not many have. I was allowed to serve the bank in ways that I didn't feel I was qualified for, but others saw my potential and gave me a chance. I learned confidence in myself, and that is one of the greatest gifts that Happy has given me. I have been allowed to work with great leaders, and I have learned so much from their examples. I have always felt respected and cared for here, and have seen what it means to have a "family" in my workplace. I have always known that Happy cared about me as an individual, and that I mattered to you and to the company. As a CEO, you have always been so approachable. I have always felt that instead of working for a company, I am working for you.

For the past three and a half years, Happy has provided me with a pleasant work atmosphere, more than enough pay, outstanding benefits, and endless opportunities for advancement. If I did not know that God was calling me to be a stay-at-home mom with my daughter, I would never leave this company.

When my husband and I lived in Amarillo, we were both working full-time and attending college full-time. We had no grants, and no help from family to pay for our tuition. My husband and I believed that if God was calling us to get our degrees, then He would provide the money for our tuition without us having to go into debt. One semester, it was about two weeks away from the registration deadline. We had enough money saved to pay for my husband's tuition, but did not have enough for mine. I prayed and told the Lord that if I needed to lay out one semester, then I would, but that I love school, and I really wanted to attend. One afternoon at work, I was visiting with a coworker who happened to mention to me that Happy has a scholarship program of $1,000/year. I inquired with HR, and was able to submit the paperwork the day before the deadline. I was given the scholarship and was able to attend school that semester, which allowed me to graduate on time. I cry every time I think about this story, because it is a perfect example of how Happy has blessed my life.

Sir, I cannot tell you "Thank you" enough.

SHEYANNE BROWN

Support Specialist

PART FOUR

NOW IT'S YOUR TURN

10

DOING WHAT YOU COULD
NEVER HAVE DONE BEFORE

By now you know that a *non-negotiable* is: A positive standard that respects the rights of others and is absolute. If you look back at the 20 Happy State Bank non-negotiables I've just shared with you, I think you'll find each and every one of them aligns with the definition above. I hope you noticed that even the non-negotiables about prayer and faith in Jesus are actually positive standards that have been carefully positioned so as to not violate anyone else's rights. Pat never *demands* that a co-owner pray or believe in Jesus. He never makes that a condition of employment. He just reserves the right to let you know, if you are a co-owner, that these are *his* values and that he personally, supports them! If you support them, too, that's great. If not, there are plenty of other places to build common ground.

Pat told me, "When I talk to new hires, I will talk about my faith, but I will also make it clear to them that there is nothing in the employee handbook that says you have to pray or go to church or do anything else that connects to your personal spirituality. This is not about everyone being a Christian. However, I do reserve the right to tell you what your CEO believes, because that's who I am!"

I've shared Pat's non-negotiables to demonstrate for you what they are, the power they can produce, and to stimulate your thinking to create your own. Imagine being able, at any given moment, being ready to explain to someone who's curious why your non-negotiables are important to you. It's not about imposing your perspectives on others. It's about defining who you are, what culture you want established, and then developing that environment. Pat has employees who *don't* share his religious beliefs, but they still understand and accept his value system, and acknowledge that his religious beliefs are part of who he is.

> **As long as we do continue to work for organizations that our beliefs do not align with, we will be disengaged at work. We will not give our best effort, we will lack meaning and purpose in our professional lives, and we will eventually question our life's purpose, mission, and beliefs. Accountability won't be nurtured. It will be diminished.**

At the end of the day, all you can really do is a) share what makes a given non-negotiable matter in your world, and b) notice who makes it their non-negotiable, too, so you can get to work on maintaining it together.

Of course, it's *nice* if someone else embraces one of your non-negotiables for themselves, but what's most important is that you value people and align your decisions with your belief system, what is in your control, your mission, and your non-negotiables *in your own world*. Having said that, though, I have to acknowledge that *most* of the co-owners of Happy State Bank I met had personally adopted each and every one of the 20 items you just read as personal non-negotiables. The principles you just read weren't opinions for these people. They were non-negotiables!

The co-owners at Happy State Bank already had the seeds of these non-negotiable items within them. Pat simply creates the environment where you can be who you really are, and he brings out the very best in people. Pat creates a place where everyone can be comfortable living their belief system, measuring against the standard that they choose to live their life, because that is exactly what Pat is doing.

Notice, too, that Pat's non-negotiables are not policy statements. None of the non-negotiables you just read about were tied to a performance outcome. They are broad statements of principle that identify the direction the bank is going, but not the vehicle used to make the journey. So for instance: You read that service is a critical, non-negotiable goal for everyone at Happy State Bank. You didn't read a non-negotiable that all messages from customers have to be returned within four hours. The first statement is a non-negotiable, the second is an outcome they want to produce. If you told someone that your non-negotiable was that everyone who works for your firm has to wear white shirts on Fridays, you'd be wrong. That's not a non-negotiable. That's a policy.

Just tacking a bunch of words to a wall accomplishes nothing for you or your organization. (It actually does more harm than good.) We've all seen companies who have spiffy mission statements and wonderful-sounding "core values" splashed across their websites. Many times these are just empty words, and we know that because of our own experiences with those companies. What happens on the front lines is not congruent with the words on the website. The people who wrote the words may have been the leadership of the organization, or the words may originate in marketing and then receive the leader's stamp of approval. When we work with these organizations, we have to clean up the issues they've created before we can move forward. The difference at Happy State Bank is that these non-negotiables existed first as expressions of *how Pat Hickman actually operates*—and *then* in the people with whom he surrounds himself.

The people in any organization have to experience someone actually *taking a stand* for a non-negotiable in a memorable way to even notice it and consider making it part of the culture cus-tomers experience on a daily basis.

Employees have to experience someone consistently and routinely *refusing to sell out the non-negotiable* in order for the non-negotiable to take root as part of the culture.

Sometimes people ask me why there are so few non-negotia-bles in our workplaces. I always say: "Not enough people getting fired, not enough companies getting fired!"

Employees have to experience someone consistently and routinely refusing to sell out the non-negotiable in order for the non-negotiable to take root as part of the culture.

Companies need to quickly let go of employees who consis-tently violate organizational non-negotiables. By the same token, if the organization you're working for consistently violates *your* non-negotiables, you need to leave the company—quickly! Unless you are willing to part company over a non-negotiable, it's not really a non-negotiable. Now I realize that this is easy to say. When you have children to support, when the house payment is due, when you feel like doing things like eating, and maybe pay-ing tuition and keeping the car, you have every right to decide you need to keep your income stream predictable.

So: Maybe the changes we need to make will take some time to plan out and make happen. We should remember as we plan, though, that as long as we do continue to work for organizations that our beliefs do not align with, we will be disengaged at work. We will not give our best effort, we will lack meaning and pur-pose in our professional lives, and we will eventually question our life's purpose, mission, and beliefs. Accountability won't be nurtured. It will be diminished.

Don't settle for a life of less—less meaning, less purpose, less sat-isfaction at home or at work. Nowhere in any doctrine is it written that we have to settle for less! We all have the right to expect more, but it's our responsibility to take the action steps in our life necessary for us to serve more, be more, and get more. Ultimately, it's our responsibility to identify and live by our own non-negotiables.

> **You must not just respect the rights of others, you must also respect their beliefs. You don't have to agree with them, but respect is critical. This process is never about getting someone to subscribe to your beliefs. Your mission isn't to get others to believe what you believe. You are working to know your non-negotiables and living your non-negotiables.**

This brings us to a big question. How do you *create* a personal non-negotiable? I've shared with you the process based on valuing people, a belief system, knowing what you can control, and a mission, but let's take it from the idea stage to the personal determination level. Let's start with you and what you really believe.

DO YOU KNOW WHAT YOU BELIEVE?

If you're like I was as I began this project, you're wondering, *"How do I know what I believe?"*

What is non-negotiable in your life always starts with your beliefs. No one will be able to create a non-negotiable unless they first know what they believe.

So let's start there. Do you know what you believe about...

- How you should treat people?
- How you run your business or perform at work?
- Delivering on your promises?
- Supporting others on your team?
- Encouraging and leading your family?

- Building relationships?
- Supporting your spouse?
- Treating and caring for your aging parents?

These are big questions. We have to take the time to understand and know what we believe in such areas of our lives. We have to make the time to think in a purposeful way about these issues, to ponder and to decide for ourselves what we believe, what our standard is based on, and whether we really are willing to take the actions necessary to live those beliefs.

> **If you commit to living your beliefs so that what you say you believe is what you really believe, your actions will align with your words—and when that happens you literally can't fail, because you are constantly moving forward toward a destination that makes sense for you.**

Happy State Bank isn't the only company that thrives because of what it believes on both the individual and organizational level. B&H Photo in New York, for instance, closes at sunset on Friday and opens again at sunset on Saturday. The Jewish owners of B&H have a belief system that says Saturday is the Sabbath and we will not work on the Sabbath. No one works. Even the website isn't available to place orders during that time frame. They pass up the biggest retail day of the week because they know what they believe and they live it. Notice that they are not ashamed of what they believe. They are open about it and more than happy to talk to anyone about it. They reserve the right in their business to run their business by how they live their life.

It's the same at the national restaurant chain Chick-Fil-A®. For S. Truett Cathy, the founder and CEO, Sunday is a day of rest, and you don't work on Sunday. That is the standard by which he lives his life—and his restaurants operate that way to this day.

No Chick-Fil-A® restaurant will ever be open on a Sunday. Even in shopping malls where stores have mandatory "open hours," all Chick-Fil-A® locations are closed on Sunday.

Many stores talk about customer service, but it's usually just rhetoric. I shop at Nordstrom, Costco, and REI because all three stores carry high quality merchandise and eagerly stand behind their products. You can return anything at any time for any reason and they take it back—no questions asked! These three stores believe that the customer should always be happy and satisfied with a product, not only when they make the purchase, but also forever. That is their belief and they support it with their actions. If a product doesn't perform to a customer's expectations they take it back, period. And they never allow you to feel less than appreciated when you return something. Many times when I've asked about how to get something repaired, with no intention of returning the item, they just offer, almost insist, on taking the item back. When you work at one of these stores, you know what the belief is, and when you are a customer you know as well.

Another part of this equation is equally critical: You must not just respect the rights of others, you must also respect their beliefs. You don't have to agree with them, but respect is critical.

This process of defining your beliefs is never about getting someone to subscribe to your beliefs. Your goal isn't to get others to believe what you believe. You are working toward knowing your non-negotiables and living your non-negotiables. You are not ashamed of your beliefs, and you will let others know what you believe when it's appropriate, but you are not trying to sway them to adopt your beliefs—nor should they try to sway you to adopt theirs!

If you commit to living your beliefs so that what you say you believe is what you really believe, your actions will align with your words—and when that happens you literally can't fail, because you are constantly moving forward toward a destination that makes sense for you. You really will gain amazing power in this process, and you had better be ready for some pretty amazing things. When you live your life by proven beliefs, you will get proven results. Pat does, the owners of B&H do, Truett Cathy does, I have, and so will you.

PUT THE TIME IN!

It takes time and energy to fully understand your own beliefs. You should make the investment in yourself by taking the time necessary to discover and affirm your beliefs. This time may involve praying, meditating, pondering, thinking—pick what works for you.

You have to know what you want to change from, in order to identify what you want to change to!

Ultimately, you are going to want to look at three areas to discover what you really believe—experiences, events, and emotional evidence. Within these areas lie the clues to the source of your beliefs—and the detail and clarity you seek.

Experiences
What personal life experiences have actually tested your stated beliefs? For instance, Pat's stated belief "Do what's right" was tested when he was told by his investors that he had to go back and renegotiate the deal with Carl Small. What has happened in your life that has supported your beliefs or caused you to question them?

In my life, the death of one of my daughter's closest friends at the age of 14 was a significant experience. Did I question my beliefs? Yes. Did I question God's participation in all of our lives? Yes. Did I question how a higher purpose could possibly be operating as we all experienced such a tragedy? You bet I did! And it took time, a lot of time, to work through the feelings and emotions of that traumatic event. I believe that there is a bigger picture that we don't get to see or fully understand, and what is needed to be revealed will be revealed to us at the right time. That belief is what allows me to accept, with difficulty sometimes, events that don't make sense at the moment.

I know what I believe and I'm able to find comfort in that, but of course that doesn't always mean that the choices or responses are easy. When a business deal doesn't go the way I want, for instance, I step back and say to myself: "All I can do is all I can do." I can believe I used all of my creativity, energy, and persistence to achieve an objective, but I know that sometimes there is just more to the story than I can see.

Events

What key events shaped your beliefs? Events that can affect our beliefs happened before we were born and continue to happen. Such an event could be the Holocaust, the Civil Rights Movement, 9/11, or even a demonstration we simply watch on television. We process our own beliefs through such big events. We look at how others acted, and then we lay our belief on top of that situation and decide for ourselves whether or not they acted properly or should have acted differently. Such events can be "good" or "bad" in nature—but they have to be big, and they have to lead to decisions that affect the way you interact with others.

When you look at an event like the Holocaust, and consider the millions of people who were killed simply because of what they believed, that kind of event causes you to think about your beliefs. It causes you to think more deeply about what is right and wrong and how you should treat other people. You will analyze your beliefs about respect, and you will analyze your beliefs about the value of all human beings differently. We all use "big" events to test, evaluate, and form beliefs.

Emotional Evidence

What evidence do you have that you were actually troubled by the prospect of acting in a way that was out of alignment with your beliefs? What evidence do you have that your beliefs served the results you support? What evidence do you have that a particular belief has "worked" for you?

In Pat's case, he could point to the fact that, before he agreed to call Carl and ask for a lower price, he *told* his investors that he was convinced that breaking his word with Carl was not the right thing to do because he trusted his belief that the Bible says the Golden Rule is a good thing. Pat always believes that "Good guys win."

We can't possibly hit a target that we can't see. When you can see the next level of what you really can be as a person and as a business professional, it becomes immensely easier to grow to that level.

So many times we have the emotional evidence right in front of us, but we fail to pay attention to it. Think about a time in your life when you knew what the right thing to do was, and yet you did something else. We all have those. The question is: *How do you feel about it now?* Maybe you thought you could get away with it, maybe you used the perceived outcome to justify the decision in your mind, or maybe you were just moving too fast to stop and listen to that part of you that really knew what the right and best decision was. Again: How do you feel about it right now?

I've looked at situations in my own life where I have said that I believe something, but my actions were not totally aligned with that stated belief. In other words I didn't really believe it, and I have worked to correct my actions. For example, it's not enough for me to say that I believe all people are created equally; I must *treat* all people with the same respect, courtesy, attention, and care.

Since beginning this adventure with Pat, I have noticed that I wasn't treating everyone the same. I noticed that I treated people with whom I had a relationship differently than someone I had just met, or someone who was providing a service like a hostess or waiter at a restaurant, someone behind the counter at a store, or maybe the person cleaning my hotel room. Sure, I was nice, or tried to be, but I didn't act the same to each of them as I would to others—and that told me I saw them differently. I teach accountability, but my friendship with Pat Hickman challenged me to live at a higher level of accountability—which is an outflow of having non-negotiables.

So now, I've changed the way I engage everyone. My goal is to show the same care, interest, and passion for connecting to absolutely everyone I come in contact with. I slow down to get to know people better. I learn more about what excites them, what challenges them, and what is going on in their life. I take the time to show my gratitude for what they do and how they contribute to my life. Yes, this is a journey. No, I know I'm not there yet. But I'm headed in the right direction.

The single act of showing intentional and conscious gratitude to everyone I come in contact with has had a huge impact in my life. Not only am I positively affecting other peoples' lives, I'm changing my own mindset and perspective for the better. This mind shift actually brings more joy and satisfaction to my day; it lifts my mood and positively affects my actions and my results.

> **Just because you say you believe something doesn't make it truth! If your actions don't support the belief then it really isn't a belief. Creating a non-negotiable is the very act of taking back control of an aspect of your life that is out of control.**

I continually receive evidence that my actions are creating different relationships than before. People react to my interest with interest of their own; the conversations we share go deeper.

The new way people interact with me is solid proof to me that my beliefs work—and it only strengthens my resolve to make certain my actions stay aligned with my beliefs. I'm amazed at the depth of the new relationships I'm building—and the personal rewards are incredible.

The actual changes in behavior I've made may seem small on the surface, but they have generated significant results. Consider this: Your current actions may be close to supporting your stated beliefs, or they could be way off. Sometimes it's easier to notice when we're way off, but either way we need to take the time to evaluate both what we believe and what we actually do. This means having conversations with ourselves with purpose, on purpose, and for a purpose. This means investing the time in ourselves, not just once, but on an ongoing basis.

Ultimately we have to decide what we believe and go with it, support it, defend it, and have faith in it. That's what believing is all about. Our beliefs must become a source of strength and a power in our lives—expressed through action. And from that will come our mission and non-negotiables—the source of true power.

IT'S TIME TO TAKE BACK CONTROL

I want to repeat a question that I posed early on in the book: What are you willing to take control of in your life, right now?

At its root, that's really what a non-negotiable is—a *choice* to maintain control over a specific area in your life.

You may have reached a point where you are *fed up* with whatever has gotten out of control. This is *reactive* establishment of a non-negotiable. Recall how Pat reached a point where he was no longer willing to overlook his personal commitment to Carl just to keep his investors happy. He'd had enough. Sometimes that's how it goes. When we are *fed up*, it may be easier to decide that something can and should change in our lives and that we must change it.

Alternatively, you may have simply reached a personal conclusion that tells you it is time to make a change and take control of a new area of your life. This is *proactive* establishment of a new non-negotiable. It may be based on having learned something new and important, perhaps as a result of having gotten some kind of feedback from your environment, or it may be based on reading a book or article that exposes you to new ideas, or you may find yourself enrolled in a group where membership is based on an acceptance of a new belief. Recall how Pat's investors adopted his belief, "Do what's right," once he established it as a non-negotiable. It may simply be that you are already in control but you want to take specific steps to stay in control.

Whether you adopt a reactive or a proactive approach, the process of changing your belief into a non-negotiable must begin with the firm decision that you are now taking control of something that has become unacceptable—a decision to officially leave behind an old worldview that told you that other people or other circumstances controlled that part of your life.

LET'S GET STARTED!

It takes sustained effort to understand your beliefs and discover what your non-negotiables are. Start the process *right now.*

Schedule private time to evaluate your life, your experiences, and your beliefs—and listen to that "still small voice" inside your head and heart. Get a clearer sense of what you were put on earth to do. Make a conscious decision to take control of a certain area of your life that is currently out of control.

If you start on this journey, you will move closer to identifying your beliefs, defining a mission, and developing non-negotiables. How do I know that? Because that's what happened to me.

MY OWN NON-NEGOTIABLE

I think back now on my relationship with Pat and Happy State Bank and I shake my head in wonder at all that has changed.

When I started this project, I saw it as a case study about a successful business applying the principles of *accountability* that I espouse and teach publicly. Very early on, though, I realized that it was a much more significant project than that. Then I thought it was going to be a book about a successful man and his bank. And while that is accurate, the learning experience turned into much more for me.

I've never met anyone who couldn't improve. Most of us have lots of room for improvement. Many times, the problem is that we don't know what's possible, or we don't even know what the next level looks like. It's hard for any of us to hit a target that we can't see. Real growth doesn't come from reading a book. Real growth comes from being real honest with yourself and where you are.

Pat showed me what really knowing what you believe is all about. He showed me the awesome power of knowing exactly what is non-negotiable in your life. He showed me how to run a business the same way you live your life. That model alone was a doctoral-level class in authenticity.

Through the writing of this book, I have been working on better understanding my own belief system, truly valuing people, knowing what is in my control, my mission and subsequent non-negotiables—and a new level of accountability. I think back to the lessons of my parents and grandparents. I think about the place in my life where my own spirituality lives, to my covenant with God, and the areas of my life where my actions have supported my stated beliefs, as well as the areas where they have not.

Ultimately I believe that we are all created in the image of God. For this reason, every person is equally important and has an infinite potential to do good in the world. In the past I would have kept this belief to myself. Now, I am unashamed to state this. My goal is to have my daily actions be totally aligned with this belief. That's now a non-negotiable for me. Before, it was something I took action on with less than total consistency.

> **To be honest, you have to be honest all of the time. To be accountable, you have to be accountable all of the time. To be genuine, you have to be genuine all of the time. If we truly believe something, then we believe it all of the time, and we act accordingly.**

One reason Pat is so great at relationships is because he does treat everyone with equal respect. My father was great at that also, and my challenge is to do the same. Good isn't good enough. In every area of our lives—home, health, work, friendships, spirituality—we must renew our efforts daily to achieve excellence.

Remember, your belief system doesn't have to be based on any formal religious doctrine. It can be based on lessons learned from any number of sources. But if you do subscribe to a specific spiritual doctrine, then it makes sense to stop and ask yourself how well your actions are aligned with, and proof of, those beliefs you claim. Do your actions all week long support the statements you make, the agreements you make, the intentions you form in the mosque, in the synagogue, at church, or anywhere else you find your beliefs? Don't say you believe something just because it's popular. Do not fall into the trap of saying one thing but allowing your actions to betray your so-called beliefs. That's an open grave just waiting for you to fall into it!

IT'S TIME TO WRITE YOUR MISSION AND NON-NEGOTIABLES

The process I have discovered—and outlined for you in this book—now has me looking at everything I do through a different lens. It also led our team to build our company's mission:

Empowering people to live accountable lives.

Our new mission provides clarity and purpose—for me and for everyone who is associated with the work we do. This new view has allowed our organization to go much deeper into what we know and believe and teach about people, accountability, and organizational development. Our actions have changed, and so have our outcomes. We are now able to serve our clients on a significantly higher level of accountability than before, and that is exciting. From this mission statement, we developed our own non-negotiables that I want to share with you.

Don't be fooled, however. This has been a difficult process. We discuss, analyze, and challenge every word in every one of our non-negotiables. We have had heated discussions on whether we are actually living them or if they are simply goals that we think would be nice to do. We hit the bull's-eye on some and miss on others, but we get back up and work to improve. We are making progress. The most meaningful and engaging conversations we have are when we discuss our non-negotiables. And through every one of those discussions we discover more about each other and we are drawn closer. It has been a difficult but incredibly rewarding journey.

NON-NEGOTIABLES FOR SAM SILVERSTEIN, INC.

1. Do the right thing.

    i. Family—Always do what's right for our family. We help each other keep that commitment.

    ii. Partners (company employees, suppliers, and clients)—We always do what's right for our partners.

    iii. Community—We participate in the community. Service is an integral part of our mission.

2. God is in our business. God will guide us. Seek counsel through specific prayer individually and together corporately. Give thanks. Show gratitude.

3. We have a supportive environment, not a competitive environment. We support each other based on their needs. We give feedback. Around the table everybody has an equal voice.

4. Get the job done and do it great. Always deliver a level of excellence.

5. Have fun. Bring a positive attitude. Create an enjoyable work environment. Laugh together.

6. Our business is built on relationships—relationships with our team, our clients, and our community. We value, contribute to, and nurture our relationships. We speak openly and honestly within our business. We contribute value to our clients beyond specific engagements.

7. Truth—We always present an honest and accurate representation of the facts. Our word is our bond.

8. Service First—We serve everyone around us. Treat others better than they expect to be treated.

9. Recognize and Celebrate—Recognize people's contributions and celebrate the future we are creating.

10. Personal development—We seek continual spiritual and organizational growth.

11. Be courageous.

12. Live life's adventure.

I've discovered so much through the journey of writing out these non-negotiables. We really can be the same in our professional life as in our personal life—and we need to be. This is where so many of us slip. To be honest, you have to be honest all of the time. To be accountable, you have to be accountable all of the time. To be genuine, you have to be genuine all of the time.

It's the same with our beliefs and the non-negotiable elements of our life that build from those beliefs. If we truly believe something, then we believe it all of the time, and we act accordingly.

"THAT'S NOT HOW I DO BUSINESS"

I was managing a piece of commercial property for my mother, and out of the blue, without any effort on my part, someone offered to purchase the property.

> It's not enough for us to just move to the next level, to better ourselves, and to be the best we can be. We shouldn't just aspire to grow to a level of greatness. We must grow to a level where we inspire greatness in the people around us.

It was a warehouse that was not in a great area and the tenants had just moved out. I knew the condition of the building was poor, and I wasn't excited about having to invest more money in a building that wasn't in a growth area of town. Bottom line: I was happy to get the offer that had come our way. Here was a great opportunity to get out of maintaining a property that was really not in my mother's best interest at this point in her life.

After seeing the building inside and out, the purchaser made us a formal offer. We agreed on the price and the details of the transaction, and then they submitted and I signed a contract. The deal was supposed to be an "as is" sale.

But then things immediately started to change. The purchaser sent an inspector out to the building and he submitted a 34-page report filled with pictures and descriptions of everything that he thought needed to be fixed. The purchaser's attorney said that there was more than $100,000 worth of work that needed to be done on the building, and unless we were willing to lower our price by $50,000, the deal was off.

The report was filled with contrived problems on a building that they had already seen inside and out before making an unsolicited offer to us. They had started out positioning themselves as unexpected angels, benevolent souls who materialized out of nowhere, and wanted only to help us out by taking a distressed property off our hands. Now, however, they were showing their true faces—bullies.

This purchaser had used a tactic: Get the building under contract and then blow every little detail that was not quite perfect out of all proportion so they could get us to "settle" on a steep discount on the agreed-upon purchase price. They were out to wear us down and even threatened litigation to get the building at a bargain-basement price that was a fraction of what we had agreed. I told my agent that the deal was off, that I didn't do business that way. I contacted my attorney and instructed him to notify the other side that we were out.

As I expected, the other side said they were going to sue for failure to comply with the agreement. My attorney said we were not at fault and the other side didn't have a leg to stand on. More to the point, it turned out that the purchaser still wanted the building. (I had expected that, too.)

I still thought that selling was in my mother's best interest.

I called my attorney and told him that the price just went up by the increased cost of the legal fees I was now incurring to handle this situation. Additionally, I wanted my attorney to add an even stricter "as is" clause to the agreement.

I instructed my attorney that before he submitted everything in writing, as a transaction like this would normally be handled, he should call the attorney from the other side and tell him, "This is not how Sam does business. If you want the building, here are the final terms. Take it or leave it, but if you counteroffer the entire deal is off. If you try to change anything, Sam will not sell you the building." (Remember Pat's non-negotiable? Do what's right!)

Those were the terms I told him to lay down. My attorney said, "I understand. You are indifferent as to whether or not you sell the building."

I answered, "No. That's not it. I would like to sell the building. This isn't about being tough, being difficult, or even playing hardball. I am not looking to make more on the deal and I am not going to take less. All I want is the deal that both sides had agreed to. Anything else is not how I do business. I have always said, 'My word is my bond.' I keep my word on what I will do and I expect them to do the same. It's the right thing to do. This is a non-negotiable in my life."

The attorney paused for a second and then said, "I completely understand. I like that."

This situation was an opportunity for me to live what I believed. It was a chance to take what I saw Pat do so well and make it an indelible part of my own life in both big events and small ones. It was an opportunity to practice what I preach, to maintain control. Notice that the attorney for the buyer was trying to gain control of me and the whole transaction. He wanted to dictate how everything would play out, and earn a sweet discount for his client with everything on his terms. However, my non-negotiable left *me* in control. Life is so much better when you live it in control!

Within five minutes my attorney called me back and told me I just sold the building. I called Pat right after that to share my story with him and he said, "The good guy always wins."

You know what? He was right. It's my belief that when you keep score over the long term, the good guy does always win. Pat Hickman is living proof of that. You and I can be, too.

GREAT ISN'T GOOD ENOUGH

Pat taught me that it's not enough to try to be the best you can be. Most people I know want to better themselves. Most people I know want to move their life or their career "to the next level." But, most people I know don't really know what the next level looks like!

Again: We can't possibly hit a target that we can't see. One of the great things I experienced being with Pat so much is that I had a front row seat in a show called "Active Dependence." That show is all about seeing exactly how great you can really be when you combine your hard work with meaningful prayer. I know that Pat will blush when he reads this and try to be modest, but that's what happened.

Thanks to Pat's ongoing example of active dependence, I went from "Why me?" (as in, "Why should this book project involve me?") to "Why me?" (as in, "How did I get to be so fortunate to have all this great information come my way?"). I experienced just what it is like to know exactly what you believe, to discover the richness of valuing people, to be able to focus on what you can control, to know your mission, to know what in your life is non-negotiable, to know what happens to your relationships when you live your life and run your business by what you believe. To know that all kinds of doors open for you once you experience possibility as an ongoing way of life. The truth is that people around Pat are better people than they imagined they could be—because Pat brings that out in everyone. He helps them to envision, with clarity, who they really want to be next. That's my goal too, to help others realize their immense potential.

When you can see the next level of what you really can be as a person and as a business professional, it becomes immensely easier to grow to that level. We need to work hard at finding what the next level looks like so that we can more quickly move there. If we just wait to run into that person, it might never happen—or worse, if we're not looking for that person, we might not recognize the moment of truth, the moment of transformation, when it rolls around.

It's not enough for us to just move to the next level, to better ourselves and to be the best we can be. We shouldn't just aspire to grow to a level of greatness. We must grow to a level where we inspire greatness in the people around us. That is the ultimate achievement in personal development—and that's what Pat Hickman does every day.

In sports, the team MVP (Most Valuable Player) is the player who not only puts up great numbers, but also the player who makes everyone around them better. Pat is the MVP. He makes everyone around him a superstar. I can't tell you how many times during an interview someone associated with Happy State Bank looked at me through red, watery eyes and said, "Pat believes in me. I do things I could have never done anywhere else. Pat has made me a better person." Pat would say the same about them. An accountable leader knows that they are better people, more successful, and achieve the results they are seeking because of the people around them.

These weren't just throwaway comments told to me by someone who was trying to suck up for their next promotion. These were statements of the heart from people who were visibly moved by the impact Pat had on their life.

So, here's the key. Pat doesn't try to change people's lives. Pat is just Pat. He knows who he is and lives his life by his beliefs. His strength of conviction empowers everyone around him to develop their own strength of conviction, and in doing that they grow to be someone they never even imagined possible.

11

WHAT'S LUCK GOT
TO DO WITH IT?

Remember the luncheon that I mentioned at the beginning of the book, the one with the 15 business leaders from Amarillo? Well, I found out over a year later, and long after I started writing this book, that Pat wasn't on the original invite list. He should have been invited, but somehow another banker from a large bank had been invited, and Sharon didn't think it would be good to have both of them present.

Funny thing: The other banker was out of town and couldn't attend. Pat ended up being invited. That luncheon was the first time Pat received a copy of my book *No More Excuses*—and guess what? That same copy was sitting on his desk when I visited his office for the very first time. That's where we had the chance to speak and connect. That's really where it all started.

So I ask you: Was I "lucky" that the other banker was out of town? Did "luck" change my fate and lead to the opportunity of a wonderful, life-changing friendship that would transform me, my whole organization, and maybe even you?

No. I wasn't lucky. Luck didn't have anything to do with that series of events.

A poster in the athletic training room of the high school I attended years ago said, "Luck is the point where preparation meets opportunity." I think back to that poster at least once a day and the message it contained. I understand what preparation is. Preparation is studying your craft, practicing, and training. Exactly what is opportunity? "Opportunity" is an ambiguous word. Where does every opportunity come from? Your answer depends on what you believe. Ultimately, I believe opportunity is nothing more or less than those open doors that Pat talked about, those doors that stay open until God closes them. They are open for Pat, they are open for me, and I believe they are open for you.

The truth is, Pat knows exactly what happened at that luncheon, and so do I. It is our belief that it was providence. It is what was supposed to happen, because I was supposed to get to know Pat and we were supposed to build a lasting friendship—and I was supposed to tell his story to you. That's what I choose to believe.

Do you know what you believe?

Do you know what in your life is non-negotiable?

MAKE IT HAPPEN IN YOUR WORLD

I once asked Pat: "If you bought a bank in the middle of a large city in another part of the country, New York City, say, could you create the same culture as you have here?"

He didn't hesitate for a moment. "Yep," he said. "Might be tough, might take some time, but you could do it."

> This isn't a fad. It's a way of living your life that will bring you the greatest rewards and the greatest riches in terms of relationships, support, influence, and the ability to change lives.

I suspected that's what he would say, but I wanted to be sure. I needed to know that there wasn't something in the water in Texas that supported people being able to live their life this way—and build a business and organizational culture based on the way they lived their life. Since then, I've confirmed that you really can do this anywhere.

I know you're wondering now whether any of this will work for you, whether you can really have that much control in your life, whether you can gain total certainty about what you believe, whether the environment *you* work in can offer trust, support and be a wonderful place to go, a place where you create the person you were meant to be, every day.

> **Once you have a non-negotiable, your course is clear. You know what kind of life you're building for yourself and what kind of culture you're building for others.**

The short answer is "yes." If one person can do it, then two can, and if two can then tens, hundreds, thousands, and even more can. But I can guarantee you that it won't be easy. If it were easy, everybody would be doing it!

Let's be honest. You will have to deal with negative people. You will have to confront change. You will have to make some very difficult decisions along the way. Our clients face these challenges on a regular basis as we step them through this process.

You will face different challenges making these changes in your personal life than in your professional life. If you are the owner of a company, your path will be different than if you are the president of a publicly traded company. If you are the president of an organization, your path will be different than if you are on the executive team. If you are on the executive team, your path will be different than if you are in middle management. If you are on the front lines, your path will be different from the path of all of those people you interact with daily.

If you are in a position of authority, you may have to fire people, or as they say at Happy, "Allow them to succeed somewhere else where that behavior is accepted." By the same token, you may have to fire your company and move some place where your voice can be heard, some place where they either already have something or already want something that is significantly better than what is happening right now. There may be several months or even several years of struggle, but you can do this. It will all come down to what you believe and what you do. If you believe that it is possible to make this change, then it is. Pat has already proved that for all of us. If you are willing to be responsible, to step up and take responsibility for what you believe and how you act, then I can promise you, your actions will take you in a new direction.

It all starts inside you. You must value people, you must determine what you believe, you must understand what you can control, you must define your mission, and you must know beyond any doubt what is non-negotiable in your life. When you set the example, then others around you will have the opportunity to follow you.

Do you know what you believe?

Are your current beliefs holding you back?

Do you know why you believe what you believe?

Each time your non-negotiables are tested and you stay the course, you will grow stronger, your non-negotiables will grow stronger, the people around you will be more supportive—and you will move closer to creating the culture and the life you're seeking.

The *why* is important, too. There was a time when people in the United States believed that a black person was only worth three fifths of a white person. That is how they were counted in the census. Some people believed that and some didn't. But it was wrong and it was changed. Just because it was believed by some didn't make it true.

- Are your beliefs sound?
- Do your beliefs respect the rights of others?
- Do your beliefs honor yourself and honor others?
- Are they based on experience?
- Can you support them in public and in private?
- Do your beliefs change when money is involved?

Questions like these show where you have to go to get to the real heart of a belief structure—a belief structure that will support the type of life and the type of culture you want to build.

When you have influence either in your family, your department, or your organization as a whole, on some important goal whose importance everyone accepts, that's when you need to start sharing with others what your beliefs, mission, and non-negotiables are. Remember, you share them through your actions and through your words. If you state a belief, mission, or non-negotiable and then don't live it, then your credibility is immediately diminished and your strength is eroded.

Once you begin down this road there is no turning back. You will not want to settle for less, you will know there is a better way ahead, and you will know that a step backward is costly. It's possible that some of the people around you will want to see you fail. Some won't understand what you are doing. They may think it's just another management or lifestyle fad. This isn't a fad. It's a way of living your life that will bring you the greatest rewards and the greatest riches in terms of relationships, support, influence, and the ability to change lives. And yes, in a business setting, it will translate directly to the bottom line.

Each time your non-negotiables are tested and you stay the course, you will grow stronger, your non-negotiables will grow stronger, the people around you will be more supportive—and you will move closer to creating the culture and the life you're seeking.

Remember my experience around the sale of that warehouse property? Through that conversation, the relationship I had with my attorney changed. I could hear a shift in his voice as he digested and understood why I was making the decisions I was making. My relationship with my real estate agent changed, as well. He even called me and asked when he could buy a copy of this book!

You will have to make some very difficult choices along the way. Some of the choices will cost you money, time, or both. This will be the point when your real convictions show. Are you willing to lose a little money in the short term to support what is non-negotiable in your life, so that you and everyone on the team can benefit in the long run? Are you willing to let go of someone in your organization who produces a lot of sales or completes an important task if they undermine a key non-negotiable, like doing the right thing? Will you treat that winning football coach the same way you treat a teacher, librarian, or other employee— or does that coach get special treatment and special privileges? Does the student who signed an oath not to drink or use any controlled substances, under the penalty of being kicked off of the team, actually get kicked off of the team for violating the agreement? Even if it's two days before the state championship? What will you do if the parents threaten to sue? What will you do if you are the parents whose kid has been thrown off the team?

What do you believe? What is non-negotiable in your life?

All of this can look very difficult, but it's actually very easy. Once you have a non-negotiable in your life, you have control— just as I had control over what could have been a messy situation with that real estate transaction. I'm not saying be non-negotiable in a stubborn or aggressive kind of way. Remember, a non-negotiable is a positive standard that respects the rights of others and is absolute. If you remember nothing else from this book, remember this: Once you have a non-negotiable, your course is clear. You know what kind of life you're building for yourself and what kind of culture you're building for others.

I've tried to give you relevant examples I could find from Pat's life, from what goes on at Happy State Bank, and from my life also. At this point, you are either going to put this book on your shelf and forget about it, or you're going to go all-in to make it happen for you and for the people who matter most to you in life. I hope it's the latter, and that within these pages you have found access to both the "why" and the "how" of the non-negotiable in your own world.

So: Do you know what you believe? Do you know what your next steps are? Now would be a great time to think about that, to start putting your thoughts down on paper, and to start this process by defining a personal mission of your own.

When you do, send it to me:
non-negotiable@samsilverstein.com

I look forward to hearing from you!

Sam Silverstein

INDEX

ABOUT THE AUTHOR

Sam Silverstein, champion of accountability, has dedicated his life to helping companies create an organizational culture that prioritizes and inspires accountability. Through his work, Sam empowers organizations to develop what they believe in, clarify their mission, and understand what is in their control, and in so doing, Sam makes this a more accountable world.

Mr. Silverstein is the author of several books including *No More Excuses* and *Making Accountable Decisions*. He speaks internationally, having worked with teams at companies, government agencies, communities, and organizations both big and small, including Kraft Foods, Pfizer, United States Air Force, and United Way. Sam is the Past President of the National Speakers Association.

SOUND WISDOM BOOKS BY SAM SILVERSTEIN

No More Excuses

Bring Non-Negotiable
To Your Organization

Sam Silverstein, Inc.
121 Bellington Lane
St. Louis, Missouri 63141
info@SamSilverstein.com
(314) 878-9252

www.twitter.com/samsilverstein
www.youtube.com/samsilverstein
www.linkedin.com/in/samsilverstein
Fax: (314) 878-1970
www.samsilverstein.com